FAVOURITE POEMS
OF THE
COUNTRYSIDE

FAVOURITE POEMS
OF THE
COUNTRYSIDE

Edited by Samuel Carr

BATSFORD

This edition first published in the United Kingdom in 2015 by

Batsford
1 Gower Street
London WC1E 6HD

An imprint of Pavilion Books Company Limited

This book is a reissue of *Ode to the Countryside* (National Trust Books, 2010)
and is based on *The Poetry of the Countryside* (Batsford, 1984)

ISBN: 9781849942928

A CIP catalogue record for this book is available from the British Library.

20 19 18 17 16 15
10 9 8 7 6 5 4 3 2 1

Printed by 1010 Printing International Ltd, China
Reproduction by Mission Productions Ltd, Hong Kong

This book can be ordered direct from the publisher at the website:
www.pavilionbooks.com, or try your local bookshop.

Contents

Introduction

'One of the great sources of poetical delight is description, or the power of presenting pictures to the mind', wrote Dr. Johnson in his life of Cowley. It is with the aim of collecting just such sources of delight that this anthology has been compiled. If nature poetry is seldom amongst the greatest that has been written there is still every reason why it should be enjoyed for its own sake. The more local and particular a poem the more suitable it will be for the present work, yet these are also the elements which are likely to set a limit to its greatness. Wordsworth's descriptive poetry 'unrolls', as Sir John Betjeman has put it, 'in great strips', but in all of it the reader is aware of the presence of the poet. Clare, by contrast, seems himself to be absent from his exactly descriptive verse and this may be one reason at least why he is a lesser poet; a lesser poet, but one who is still irreplaceable for what he uniquely wrote.

Poetry about the countryside has a long and distinguished ancestry. John Dyer's *The Fleece* and Vita Sackville-West's *The Land*, nearly two hundred years apart as they are, both had earlier models in the idylls of Theocritus and the eclogues of Virgil. It is still true, however, that a rural theme was uncommon until its introduction by Gray, Cowper and Crabbe, while afterwards it was to become increasingly popular throughout the nineteenth century. For this change the Romantic movement was in part responsible, even if Romantic painters and poets were inclined to deal more with unparticularised generalities, in the manner of so many of Turner's landscapes, than with the minuteness and precision of a later artist like W. H. Hunt. The Industrial Revolution also had its influence in the often sentimental attraction it induced towards the country and away from the dehumanising horrors of so much urban living. There was a certain irony here in that, at the same time as the middle classes were being drawn to the country, it was the prospects for the labouring classes of employment in the new factories which largely brought about the expansion of the towns.

Marxist writers might criticise a collection such as this because the poets who are represented in it were rather seldom true countrymen, more seldom still country labourers. Worse, they were most often visiting members of the bourgeoisie. Against the Rev. Stephen Duck, who began life as an agricultural labourer in Wiltshire, or Robert Bloomfield, who had worked as a shoemaker, there is a long list of much greater country poets who were able to write because of the security given them by a steady outside income, earned or unearned. Even William Barnes, that quintessential Dorset poet, was employed in a solicitor's office and as a schoolmaster. There would be no difficulty in getting together a collection of (from this point of view) impeccably genuine country poetry, but, as Rayner Unwin makes all too clear in *The Rural Muse*, it would be of sadly inferior quality.

In painting as in poetry a preoccupation with the countryside was in England a phenomenon principally of the nineteenth century (in the Low Countries it was a different matter. The landscape element in a picture like Rubens' miraculous *The Rainbow* seems to have anticipated Constable by nearly two centuries).

In the years since the First World War nature poetry as a theme has become decreasingly popular. Frances Cornford and Vita Sackville-West have indeed been succeeded by, for example, Sir John Betjeman, Norman Nicholson and Seamus Heaney, but none of these poets is, it goes without saying, of the same stature as a Hardy, much less a Wordsworth. It is less necessary to explain this change in poetic taste than it is to account for the fact that, in contrast to the hundreds of years during which poetry has been written, nature poetry should really have flourished for only a century or two. Whatever the explanation may be, the editor of this collection would like to hope that (to quote Johnson again, this time in his life of Waller) the poets who are represented in it will give delight by their descriptions of 'the beauty and grandeur of nature, the flowers of the Spring, and the harvests of Autumn, the vicissitudes of the tide and the revolutions of the Sky...'

Foreword

Landscape and love

'Landscape' covers a multitude of meanings – from coast to clough, from deep valley to high bleak moor. Likewise, of course, the word 'poetry', which encompasses so many traditions of writing about the land and its inhabitants. But they have some things in common: we turn to the land, and also to poetry to stretch our imaginations, to find space to think; to look more closely at the world than usual. We read poems as we might take a walk in the country, to escape from the daily anxieties of work and the built environment. We use both to help us enjoy a broader and fresher life – and perhaps even to indulge in a little harmless nostalgia, for a world that never was.

Poetry about the countryside has mostly been written by educated townsfolk. After all, it's easy to be romantic about the work of the ruddy-faced milkmaid when it's not you that has to get up at five o'clock to milk the ruddy cows. Alexander Pope, celebrated literary lion, would surely have been horrified if anyone had actually taken him up on his cry:

> Thus let me live, unseen, unknown,
> Thus unlamented let me die

But sometimes the rural swain takes up a pen and writes his own story, with the close observation that betrays a deep knowledge. John Clare wrote about his native Northamptonshire with precision and joy. Robert Bloomfield, sent to work in London because he was too frail for fieldwork in his native Suffolk, became a bestseller with his poems of rural life. Like him, the urban audience was gasping for fresh air – an appetite which has never faded.

Landscape makes us powerfully aware of this, and other appetites. Anyone who has welcomed the spring after a long winter can share Vita Sackville-West's sneaking adult pleasure in 'the rich warm-blood rush/ Of growth, and mating beasts, and rising sap.' After all, we share the landscape with other life forms who know it much better than we do –

'Bird and beetle, man and mole' as George Meredith has it – and with all of them, we share the weather. Once outside, weather is no longer the barely noticed patch of sky we see from the office window. It hangs the sky with clouds or sun, cools the skin with gentle breezes or whips it with snowstorms. Only outside can we be so exhilaratingly conscious of our physical selves.

Taken mostly from an age before Ted Hughes' brooding realism or Norman MacCaig's precise, head-cocking observations of birds and animals, the poetry in this collection sits comfortably in the tradition of Romantic celebration. The poems all speak of the open air, of weather-beaten skin and the sensuality of nature. Implicit in all this is the absence of the city the poet has left behind. Many of these poems are 'reports from abroad' for urban readers, reminding them that sweeter things lie outside the city limits. George Meredith cocks an ear and says with a wink:

O hear them, deep in the songless City!

In places that we know well, there is a twin feeling of belonging and of ownership. It is a complicated pride, expressed by Elizabeth Barrett Browning when she says that 'I thought my father's land was worthy too/ Of being my Shakespeare's'.

That deep-rooted love of place is at the heart of our experience when we step outside. Any list of great landscapes in Britain will include the broad uplands, rugged coasts and designed landscapes, all of which are constantly under threat from the expanding cities and their polluted air. We know now just how deep is the threat to those landscapes, and how hard we must work to conserve them. Perhaps we should enjoy them all the more for that; and they are still, as Bernard Barton rightly says:

a grateful poet's favourite theme.

Jo Bell, Poet
Cheshire, February, 2010

Living in
the Country

The Life of a Homely Swain

from: Henry VI, Part III

O God! methinks it were a happy life
To be no better than a homely swain:
To sit upon a hill, as I do now,
To carve out dials quaintly point by point,
Thereby to see the minutes, how they run:
How many make the hour full complete,
How many hours bring about the day,
How many days will finish up the year,
How many years a mortal man may live.
When this is known, then to divide the times:
So many hours must I tend my flock;
So many hours must I take my rest;
So many hours must I contemplate;
So many hours must I sport myself;
So many days my ewes have been with young;
So many weeks ere the poor fools will yean;
So many years ere I shall shear the fleece:
So minutes, hours, days, months and years,
Pass'd over to the end they were created,
Would bring white hairs unto a quiet grave.

Ah, what a life were this, how sweet, how lovely!
Gives not the hawthorn bush a sweeter shade
To shepherds, looking on their silly sheep,
Than doth a rich embroider'd canopy
To kings, that fear their subjects' treachery?
O yes it doth; a thousand-fold it doth.
And to conclude; the shepherd's homely curds,
His cool thin drink out of his leather bottle,
His wonted sleep under a fresh tree's shade,
All which secure and sweetly he enjoys,
Is far beyond a prince's delicates,
His viands sparkling in a golden cup,
His body couched in a curious bed,
When care, mistrust, and treason wait on him.

William Shakespeare
(1564–1616)

The Quiet Life

Happy the man whose wish and care
    A few paternal acres bound,
Content to breath his native air
    In his own ground.

Whose herds with milk, whose fields with bread,
    Whose flocks supply him with attire,
Whose trees in summer yield him shade,
    In winter fire.

Blest who can unconcern'dly find
    Hours, days and years slide soft away,
In health of body, peace of mind,
    Quiet by day,

Sound sleep by night; study and ease,
    Together mixt; sweet recreation;
And innocence, which most does please
    With meditation.

Thus let me live, unseen, unknown,
    Thus unlamented let me die,
Steal from the world, and not a stone
    Tell where I lie.

Alexander Pope
(1688–1744)

Invitation to the Country

Now 'tis Spring on wood and wold,
Early Spring that shivers with cold,
But gladdens, and gathers, day by day,
A lovelier hue, a warmer ray,
A sweeter song, a dearer ditty;
Ouzel and throstle, new-mated and gay,
Singing their bridals on every spray–
Oh, hear them, deep in the songless City!
Cast off the yoke of toil and smoke,
As Spring is casting winter's grey,
As serpents cast their skins away:
And come, for the Country awaits thee with pity
And longs to bathe thee in her delight,
And take a new joy in thy kindling sight;
And I no less, by day and night,
Long for thy coming, and watch for, and wait thee,
And wonder what duties can thus belate thee.

Dry-fruited firs are dropping their cones,
And vista'd avenues of pines
Take richer green, give fresher tones,
As morn after morn the glad sun shines.

Primrose tufts peep over the brooks,
Fair faces amid moist decay!
The rivulets run with the dead leaves at play,
The leafless elms are alive with the rooks.

Over the meadows the cowslips are springing,
The marshes are thick with king-cup gold,
Clear is the cry of the lambs in the fold,
The skylark is singing, and singing, and singing.

Soon comes the cuckoo when April is fair,
And her blue eye the brighter the more it may weep:
The frog and the butterfly wake from their sleep,
Each to its element, water and air.

Mist hangs still on every hill,
And curls up the valleys at eve; but noon
Is fullest of Spring; and at midnight the moon
Gives her westering throne to Orion's bright zone,
As he slopes o'er the darkened world's repose;
And a lustre in eastern Sirius glows.

Come, in the season of opening buds;
Come, and molest not the otter that whistles
Unlit by the moon, 'mid the wet winter bristles
Of willow, half-drowned in the fattening floods.
Let him catch his cold fish without fear of a gun,
And the stars shall shield him, and thou wilt shun!
And every little bird under the sun
Shall know that the bounty of Spring doth dwell
In the winds that blow, in the waters that run,
And in the breast of man as well.

George Meredith
(1828–1909)

His Content in the Country

from: Hesperides

Here, here I live with what my Board,
Can with the smallest cost afford.
Though ne'r so mean the Viands be,
They well content my Prew and me.
Or Pea, or Bean, or Wort, or Beet,
What ever comes, content makes sweet:
Here we rejoyce, because no Rent
We pay for our poore Tenement:
Wherein we rest, and never feare
The Landlord, or the Usurer.
The Quarter-day do's ne'r affright
Our Peacefull slumbers in the night.
We eate our own, and batten more,
Because we feed on no mans score:
But pitie those, whose flanks grow great,
Swel'd with the Lard of others meat.
We blesse our Fortunes, when we see
Our own beloved privacie:
And like our living, where w'are known
To very few, or else to none.

Robert Herrick
(1591–1674)

This Lime-tree Bower my Prison

Well, they are gone, and here must I remain,
This lime-tree bower my prison! I have lost
Beauties and feelings, such as would have been
Most sweet to my remembrance even when age
Had dimmed mine eyes to blindness! They, meanwhile,
Friends, whom I never more may meet again,
On springy heath, along the hill-top edge,
Wander in gladness, and wind down, perchance,
To that still roaring dell, of which I told;
The roaring dell, o'erwooded, narrow, deep,
And only speckled by the mid-day sun;
Where its slim trunk the ash from rock to rock
Flings arching like a bridge; – that branchless ash,
Unsunned and damp, whose few poor yellow leaves
Ne'er tremble in the gale, yet tremble still,
Fanned by the water-fall! and there my friends
Behold the dark green file of long lank weeds,
That all at once (a most fantastic sight!)
Still nod and drip beneath the dripping edge
Of the blue clay-stone.

               Now, my friends emerge
Beneath the wide wide Heaven – and view again
The many-steepled tract magnificent
Of hilly fields and meadows, and the sea,
With some fair bark, perhaps, whose sails light up
The slip of smooth clear blue betwixt two Isles
Of purple shadow! Yes! they wander on
In gladness all; but thou, methinks, most glad,
My gentle-hearted Charles! for thou hast pined

And hungered after Nature, many a year,
In the great City pent, winning thy way
With sad yet patient soul, through evil and pain
And strange calamity! Ah! slowly sink
Behind the western ridge, thou glorious Sun!
Shine in the slant beams of the sinking orb,
Ye purple heath-flowers! richlier burn, ye clouds!
Live in the yellow light, ye distant groves!
And kindle, thou blue Ocean! So my friend
Struck with deep joy may stand, as I have stood,
Silent with swimming sense; yea, gazing round
On the wide landscape, gaze till all doth seem
Less gross than bodily; and of such hues
As veil the Almighty Spirit, when yet he makes
Spirits perceive his presence.

                          A delight
Comes sudden on my heart, and I am glad
As I myself were there! Nor in this bower,
This little lime-tree bower, have I not marked
Much that has soothed me. Pale beneath the blaze
Hung the transparent foliage; and I watched
Some broad and sunny leaf, and loved to see
The shadow of the leaf and stem above
Dappling its sunshine! And that walnut-tree
Was richly tinged, and a deep radiance lay
Full on the ancient ivy, which usurps
Those fronting elms, and now, with blackest mass
Makes their dark branches gleam a lighter hue
Through the late twilight: and though now the bat
Wheels silent by, and not a swallow twitters,

Yet still the solitary humble-bee
Sings in the bean-flower! Henceforth I shall know
That Nature ne'er deserts the wise and pure;
No plot so narrow, be but Nature there,
No waste so vacant, but may well employ
Each faculty of sense, and keep the heart
Awake to Love and Beauty! and sometimes
'Tis well to be bereft of promised good,
That we may lift the soul, and contemplate
With lively joy the joys we cannot share.
My gentle-hearted Charles! when the last rook
Beat its straight path along the dusky air
Homewards, I blest it! deeming its black wing
(Now a dim speck, now vanishing in light)
Had crossed the mighty Orb's dilated glory,
While thou stood'st gazing; or, when all was still,
Flew creeking o'er thy head, and had a charm
For thee, my gentle-hearted Charles, to whom
No sound is dissonant which tells of Life.

Samuel Taylor Coleridge
(1772–1834)

The Happy Countryman

Who can live in heart so glad
As the merry country lad?
Who upon a fair green balk
May at pleasure sit and walk,
And amid the azure skies
See the morning sun arise, –
While he hears in every spring
How the birds do chirp and sing:
Or before the hounds in cry
See the hare go stealing by:
Or along the shallow brook,
Angling with a baited hook,
See the fishes leap and play
In a blessëd sunny day:
Or to hear the partridge call,
Till she have her covey all:
Or to see the subtle fox,
How the villain plies the box:
After feeding on his prey,
How he closely sneaks away,
Through the hedge and down the furrow
Till he gets into his burrow:
Then the bee to gather honey,
And the little black-haired coney,
On a bank for sunny place,
With her forefeet wash her face:
Are not these, with thousand moe
Than the courts of kings do know,
The true pleasing spirit's sights
That may breed true love's delights? ...

Nicholas Breton
(1545–1626)

I Wandered Lonely as a Cloud

I wandered lonely as a cloud
That floats on high o'er vales and hills,
When all at once I saw a crowd,
A host, of golden daffodils;
Beside the lake, beneath the trees,
Fluttering and dancing in the breeze.

Continuous as the stars that shine
And twinkle on the Milky Way,
They stretched in never-ending line
Along the margin of a bay:
Ten thousand saw I at a glance,
Tossing their heads in sprightly dance.

The waves beside them danced, but they
Out-did the sparkling waves in glee:
A poet could not but be gay,
In such a jocund company:
I gazed – and gazed – but little thought
What wealth the show to me had brought:

For oft, when on my couch I lie
In vacant or in pensive mood,
They flash upon that inward eye
Which is the bliss of solitude;
And then my heart with pleasure fills,
And dances with the daffodils.

William Wordsworth
(1770–1850)

Country People

from: *Lincolnshire Remembered*

So, as it darkens, leave the farm to rest,
My lingering thoughts, in quiet on the plain.
There autumn winds grow cold, and by the gate
A scythe hangs waiting in a sycamore tree.
But not man who heaves along the road
In corduroys, cares what the shadows hide.
For country people know, though they have not read,
And need no emblem of mortality.
The lichen on the grave-stones and the roofs,
November sleet, the smell of the church aisle
Speak without words, and in their hearts they hear:
Sceptre and crown must tumble down, these say,
And come at last in the cold, earthen clay
To equal the poor crooked scythe and spade.

Nor, if they have finished work, are they afraid.

Frances Cornford
(1886–1960)

Rural Privacy

Though Clock,
To tell how night drawes hence, I've none,
A Cock
I have, to sing how day drawes on.
I have
A maid (my Prew) by good luck sent,
To save
That little Fates me gave or lent.
A Hen
I keep, which creeking day by day,
Tells when
She goes her long white egg to lay.
A Goose
I have, which, with a jealous eare,
Lets loose
Her tongue, to tell what danger's neare.
A Lamb
I keep (tame) with my morsells fed,
Whose Dam
An Orphan left him (lately dead.)
A Cat
I keep, that playes about my House,
Grown fat
With eating many a miching Mouse.
To these
A Trasy I do keep, whereby
I please
The more my rurall privacie:
Which are
But toyes, to give my heart some ease:
Where care
None is, slight things do lightly please.

Robert Herrick
(1591–1674)

Village Life a Life of Pain

from: The Village

I grant indeed that fields, and flocks have charms
For him that grazes or for him that farms;
But when amid such pleasing scenes I trace
The poor laborious natives of the place,
And see the midday sun, with fervid ray,
On their bare heads and dewy temples play,
While some, with feebler heads and fainter hearts,
Deplore their fortune, yet sustain their parts –
Then shall I dare these real ills to hide
In tinsel trappings of poetic pride?

Lo! where the heath, with withering brake grown o'er,
Lends the light turf that warms the neighbouring poor;
From thence a length of burning sand appears,
Where the thin harvest waves its withered ears;
Rank weeds, that every art and care defy,
Reign o'er the land and rob the blighted rye;
There thistles stretch their prickly arms afar,
And to the ragged infant threaten war;
There poppies, nodding, mock the hope of toil;
There the blue bugloss paints the sterile soil;
Hardy and high, above the slender sheaf,
The slimy mallow waves her silky leaf;
O'er the young shoot the charlock throws a shade,
And clasping tares cling round the sickly blade;
With mingled tints the rocky coasts abound,
And a sad splendour vainly shines around.

No longer truth, though shown in verse, disdain,
But own the Village Life a life of pain.

George Crabbe
(1754–1832)

The Farm Labourer

from: The Farmer's Boy

On Giles, and such as Giles, the labour falls,
To strew the frequent load where hunger calls.
On driving gales sharp hail indignant flies,
And sleet, more irksome still, assails his eyes;
Snow clogs his feet; or if no snow is seen,
The field with all its juicy store to screen,
Deep goes the frost, till every root is found
A rolling mass of ice upon the ground.
No tender ewe can break her nightly fast,
Nor heifer strong begin the cold repast,
Till Giles with ponderous beetle foremost go,
And scattering splinters fly at every blow:
When pressing round him eager for the prize,
From their mix'd breath warm exhalations rise.

   Though night approaching bids for rest prepare,
Still the flail echoes through the frosty air;
Nor stops till deepest shades of darkness come,
Sending at length the weary labourer home.
From him, with bed and nightly food supplied,
Throughout the yard, housed round on every side,
Deep-plunging cows, their rustling feast enjoy,
And snatch sweet mouthfuls from the passing boy,
Who moves unseen beneath his trailing load,
Fills the tall racks, and leaves a scatter'd road;
Where oft the swine from ambush warm and dry,
Bolt out, and scamper headlong to their sty,
When Giles, with well-known voice, already there,
Deigns them a portion of his evening care.

Robert Bloomfield
(1766–1823)

An Unkindly May

A shepherd stands by a gate in a white smock-frock:
He holds the gate ajar, intently counting his flock.

The sour spring wind is blurting boisterous-wise,
And bears on it dirty clouds across the skies;
Plantation timbers creak like rusty cranes,
And pigeons and rooks, dishevelled by late rains,
Are like gaunt vultures, sodden and unkempt,
And song-birds do not end what they attempt:
The buds have tried to open, but quite failing
Have pinched themselves together in their quailing.
The sun frowns whitely in eye-trying flaps
Through passing cloud-holes, mimicking audible taps.
'Nature, you're not commendable to-day!'
I think. 'Better to-morrow!' she seems to say.

That shepherd still stands in that white smock-frock,
Unnoting all things save the counting his flock.

Thomas Hardy
(1840–1928)

The Farmer's Crop Ruined

from: Agriculture

Now with enraptur'd eye,
The end of all his toil, and its reward,
The farmer views. Ah, gracious Heaven! attend
His fervent prayer; restrain the tempest's rage,
The dreadful blight disarm; nor in one blast
The products of the labouring year destroy!
Yet vain is Heaven's indulgence; for when now
In ready ranks th'impatient reapers stand,
Arm'd with the scythe or sickle: – echoes shrill
Of winding horns, the shouts and hallooings loud
Of huntsmen, and the cry of opening hounds,
Float in the gale melodious, but invade
His frighted sense with dread. Near and more near
Th' unwelcome sounds approach; and sudden o'er
His fence the tall stag bounds: in close pursuit
The hunter train, on many a noble steed,
Undaunted follow; while the eager pack
Burst unresisted thro' the yielding hedge.
In vain, unheard, the wretched hind exclaims:
The ruin of his crop in vain laments:
Deaf to his cries, they traverse the ripe field
In cruel exultation; trampling down
Beneath their feet, in one short moment's sport,
The peace, the comfort of his future year.

Robert Dodsley
(1703–1764)

Working in
the Country

The Angler's Wish

I in these flowry Meades wo'd be:
These Christal streams should solace me;
To whose harmonious bubling noise,
I with my Angle wo'd rejoice,
Sit here and see the Turtle-dove,
Court his chaste Mate to acts of love,
Or on that bank feel the West wind
Breathe health and plenty, please my mind
To see sweet dew-drops kisse these flowers,
And then washt off by April-showers:
Here hear my Clora sing a song,
There see a Black-bird feed her young,
Or a Leverock build her nest;
Here give my weary spirits rest,
And raise my low-pitcht thoughts above
Earth, or what poor mortals love:
    Thus free from law-suits, and the noise
    Of Princes Courts I wo'd rejoice.

Or with my Bryan, and a book,
Loyter long dayes near Shawford-brook;
There sit by him, and eat my meat,
There see the Sun both rise and set:
There bid good morning to next day,
There meditate my time away:
    And angle on, and beg to have
    A quiet passage to a welcome grave.

Izaak Walton
(1593–1683)

The Mowers

from: Upon Appleton House

No Scene that turns with Engines strange
Does oftner then these Meadows change.
For when the Sun the Grass hath vext,
The tawny Mowers enter next;
Who seem like Israelites to be,
Walking on foot through a green Sea.
To them the Grassy Deeps divide,
And crowd a Lane to either Side.

With whistling Sithe, and Elbow strong,
These Massacre the Grass along:
While one, unknowing, carves the Rail,
Whose yet unfeather'd Quils her fail.
The Edge all bloody from its Brest
He draws, and does his stroke detest;
Fearing the Flesh untimely mow'd
To him a Fate as black forbode.

Unhappy Birds! what does it boot
To build below the Grasses Root;
When Lowness is unsafe as Hight,
And Chance o'retakes what scapeth spight?
And now your Orphan Parents Call
Sounds your untimely Funeral.
Death-Trumpets creak in such a Note,
And 'tis the Sourdine in their Throat.

Or sooner hatch or higher build:
The Mower now commands the Field;
In whose new Traverse seemeth wrought
A Camp of Battail newly fought:
Where, as the Meads with Hay, the Plain
Lyes quilted ore with Bodies slain:
The Women that with forks it fling,
Do represent the Pillaging.

And now the careless Victors play,
Dancing the Triumphs of the Hay;
Where every Mowers wholesome Heat
Smells like an Alexanders sweat.
Their Females fragrant as the Mead
Which they in Fairy Circles tread:
When at their Dances End they kiss,
Their new-made Hay not sweeter is.

Andrew Marvell
(1591–1674)

The Farmer

from: Hesperides

Then to thy corn-fields thou dost goe,
Which though well soyl'd, yet thou dost know,
That the best compost for the Lands
Is the wise Masters Feet, and Hands.
There at the Plough thou find'st thy Teame,
With a Hind whistling there to them:
And cheer'st them up, by singing how
The Kingdoms portion is the Plow.
This done, then to th' enameld Meads
Thou go'st; and as thy foot there treads,
Thou seest a present God-like Power
Imprinted in each Herbe and Flower:
And smell'st the breath of great-ey'd Kine,
Sweet as the blossomes of the Vine.
Here thou behold'st thy large sleek Neat
Unto the Dew-laps up in meat:
And, as thou look'st, the wanton Steere,
The Heifer, Cow, and Oxe draw neere
To make a pleasing pastime there.
These seen thou go'st to view thy flocks
Of sheep, (safe from the Wolfe and Fox)
And find'st their bellies there as full
Of short sweet grasse, as backs with wool.

Robert Herrick
(1591–1674)

The Dairymaid

My favourite Patty, in her dairy's pride,
Revisit; and the generous steeds which grace
The pastures of her swain, well-pleas'd, survey.
The lowing kine, see, at their custom'd hour,
Wait the returning pail. The rosy maid,
Crouching beneath their side, in copious streams
Exhausts the swelling udder. Vessels large
And broad, by the sweet hand of neatness clean'd,
Mean while, in decent order rang'd appear,
The milky treasure, strain'd thro' filtering lawn,
Intended to receive. At early day,
Sweet slumber shaken from her opening lids,
My lovely Patty to her dairy hies:
There from the surface of expanded bowls
She skims the floating cream, and to her churn
Commits the rich consistence; nor disdains,
Though soft her hand, tho' delicate her frame,
To urge the rural toil; fond to obtain
The country-housewife's humble name and praise.
Continu'd agitation separates soon
The unctuous particles; with gentler strokes
And artful, soon they coalesce: at length,
Cool water pouring from the limpid spring
Into a smooth-glaz'd vessel, deep and wide,
She gathers the loose fragments to an heap;
Which in the cleansing wave well-wrought, and press'd
To one consistent golden mass, receives
The sprinkled seasoning, and of pats, or pounds,
The fair impression, the neat shape assumes.

Robert Dodsley
(1703–1764)

Milking Time

from: The Farmer's Boy

The clatt'ring Dairy-Maid immers'd in steam,
Singing and scrubbing midst her milk and cream,
Bawls out, "Go fetch the Cows!" – he hears no more;
For pigs, and ducks, and turkeys, throng the door,
And sitting hens, for constant war prepar'd;
A concert strange to that which late he heard.
Straight to the meadow then he whistling goes;
With well-known halloo calls his lazy Cows:
Down the rich pasture heedlessly they graze,
Or hear the summon with an idle gaze;
For well they know the cow-yard yields no more
Its tempting fragrance, nor its wintry store.
Reluctance marks their steps, sedate and slow;
The right of conquest all the law they know;
The strong press on, the weak by turns succeed,
And one superior always takes the lead;
Is ever foremost, wheresoe'er they stray;
Allow'd precedence, undisputed sway;
With jealous pride her station is maintain'd,
For many a broil that post of honour gain'd.
At home, the yard affords a grateful scene;
For Spring makes e'en a miry cow-yard clean.
Thence from its chalky bed behold convey'd
The rich manure that drenching Winter made,
Which pil'd near home, grows green with many a weed,
A promis'd nutriment for Autumn's seed.
Forth comes the Maid, and like the morning smiles;
The Mistress too, and follow'd close by Giles.
A friendly tripod forms their humble seat,
With pails bright scour'd, and delicately sweet.

Where shadowing elms obstruct the morning ray,
Begins the work, begins the simple lay;
The full-charg'd udder yields its willing streams,
While Mary sings some lover's amorous dreams.

Robert Bloomfield
(1766–1823)

Hay-makers

from: *The Thresher's Labour*

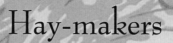

The Grass again is spread upon the Ground,
Till not a vacant Place is to be found;
And while the parching Sun-beams on it shine
The Hay-makers have Time allow'd to dine.
That soon dispatch'd, they still sit on the Ground;
And the brisk Chat, renew'd, afresh goes round.
All talk at once; but seeming all to fear,
That what they speak, the rest will hardly hear;
Till by degrees so high their Notes they strain,
A Stander-by can nought distinguish plain.
So loud's their Speech, and so confus'd their Noise,
Scarce puzzled ECHO can return the Voice.
Yet, spite of this, they bravely all go on;
Each scorns to be, or seem to be, outdone.
Mean-while the changing Sky begins to lour,

And hollow Winds proclaim a sudden Show'r;
The tattling Croud can scarce their Garments gain,
Before descends the thick impetuous Rain;
Their noisy Prattle all at once is done,
And to the Hedge they soon for Shelter run.

Thus have I seen, on a bright Summer's Day
On some green Brake, a Flock of Sparrows play;
From Twig to Twig, from Bush to Bush they fly;
And with continued Chirping fill the Sky:
But, on a sudden, if a Storm appears
Their chirping Noise no longer dins our Ears;
They fly for Shelter to the thickest Bush;
There silent sit, and all at once is hush.

Stephen Duck
(1705–1756)

The Harriers

from: The Seasons: Autumn

Poor is the triumph o'er the timid hare!
Scared from the corn, and now to some lone seat
Retired: the rushy fen; the rugged furze,
Stretch'd o'er the stony heath; the stubble chapp'd;
The thistly lawn; the thick-entangled broom;
Of the same friendly hue, the wither'd fern;
The fallow ground laid open to the sun,
Concoctive; and the nodding sandy bank,
Hung o'er the mazes of the mountain brook.
Vain is her best precaution; though she sits
Conceal'd, with folded ears; unsleeping eyes,
By Nature raised to take th' horizon in;
And head couch'd close betwixt her hairy feet,
In act to spring away. The scented dew
Betrays her early labyrinth; and deep,
In scatter'd sullen openings, far behind,
With every breeze she hears the coming storm.

But nearer, and more frequent, as it loads
The sighing gale, she springs amazed, and all
The savage soul of game is up at once:
The pack full opening, various; the shrill horn
Resounded from the hills; the neighing steed,
Wild for the chase; and the loud hunter's shout;
O'er a weak, harmless, flying creature, all
Mix'd in mad tumult and discordant joy.

James Thomson
(1700–1748)

The Thresher

from: The Task

Between the upright shafts of those tall elms
We may discern the thresher at his task.
Thump after thump, resounds the constant flail,
That seems to swing uncertain, and yet falls
Full on the destin'd ear. Wide flies the chaff;
The rustling straw sends up a frequent mist
Of atoms, sparkling in the noon-day beam.

William Cowper
(1731–1800)

Shooting, Coursing and Fishing

from: Windsor-forest

See! from the brake the whirring pheasant springs,
And mounts exulting on triumphant wings:
Short is his joy; he feels the fiery wound,
Flutters in blood, and panting beats the ground.
Ah! what avail his glossy, varying dyes,
His purple crest, and scarlet-circled eyes,
The vivid green his shining plumes unfold,
His painted wings, and breast that flames with gold?
Nor yet, when moist *Arcturus* clouds the sky,
The woods and fields their pleasing toils deny.
To plains with well-breath'd beagles we repair,
And trace the mazes of the circling hare:
(Beasts, urg'd by us, their fellow beasts pursue,
And learn of man each other to undo.)
With slaught'ring guns th'unweary fowler roves,
When frosts have whiten'd all the naked groves;
Where doves in flocks the leafless trees o'ershade,
And lonely woodcocks haunt the wat'ry glade.
He lifts the tube, and levels with his eye;
Strait a short thunder breaks the frozen sky:
Oft', as in airy rings they skim the heath,
The clam'rous plovers feel the leaden death:

Oft', as the mounting larks their notes prepare,
They fall, and leave their little lives in air.

　　In genial spring, beneath the quiv'ring shade,
Where cooling vapours breathe along the mead,
The patient fisher takes his silent stand,
Intent, his angle trembling in his hand;
With looks unmoved, he hopes the scaly breed,
And eyes the dancing cork, and bending reed.
Our plenteous streams a various race supply,
The bright-ey'd perch with fins of *Tyrian* dye,
The silver eel, in shining volumes roll'd
The yellow carp, in scales bedrop'd with gold,
Swift trouts, diversify'd with crimson stains,
And pykes, the tyrants of the watry plains.

Alexander Pope
(1688–1744)

The Village Schoolmistress

from: The Borough

To every class we have a School assign'd,
Rules for all ranks and food for every mind:
Yet one there is, that small regard to rule
Or study pays, and still is deem'd a School:
That, where a deaf, poor, patient widow sits,
And awes some thirty infants as she knits;
Infants of humble, busy wives, who pay

Some trifling price for freedom through the day:
At this good matron's hut the children meet,
Who thus becomes the mother of the street:
Her room is small, they cannot widely stray, –
Her threshold high, they cannot run away:
Though deaf, she sees the rebel-heroes shout, –
Though lame, her white rod nimbly walks about;
With band of yarn she keeps offenders in,
And to her gown the sturdiest rogue can pin:
Aided by these and spells, and tell-tale birds,
Her power they dread and reverence her words.

George Crabbe
(1754–1832)

Ploughing and Harrowing

from: The Farmer's Boy

No wheels support the diving, pointed, share;
No groaning ox is doom'd to labour there;
No helpmates teach the docile steed his road;
(Alike unknown the ploughboy and his goad;)
But, unassisted through each toilsome day,
With smiling brow the ploughman cleaves his way,
Draws his fresh parallels, and, wid'ning still,
Treads slow and heavy dale, or climbs the hill:
Strong on the wing his busy followers play,
Where writhing earth-worms meet th' unwelcome day;
Till all is chang'd, and hill and level down
Assume a livery of sober brown:
Again disturb'd, when Giles with wearying strides
From ridge to ridge the ponderous harrow guides;
His heels deep sinking every step he goes,
Till dirt adhesive loads his clouted shoes.
Welcome green headland! firm beneath his feet;
Welcome the friendly bank's refreshing seat;
There, warm with toil, his panting horses browse
Their shelt'ring canopy of pendent boughs;
Till rest, delicious, chase each transient pain,
And new-born vigour swell in every vein.

Robert Bloomfield
(1766–1823)

Harry Ploughman

Hard as hurdle arms, with a broth of goldish flue
Breathed round; the rack of ribs; the scooped flank; lank
Rope-over thigh; knee-nave; and barrelled shank –
      Head and foot, shoulder and shank –
By a grey eye's heed steered well, one crew, fall to;
Stand at stress. Each limb's barrowy brawn, his thew
That onewhere curded, onewhere sucked or sank –
      Soared or sank – ,
Though as a beechbole firm, finds his, as at a roll-call, rank
And features, in flesh, what deed he each must do –
      His sinew-service where do.

He leans to it, Harry bends, look. Back, elbow, and liquid waist
In him, all quail to the wallowing o' the plough: 's cheek crimsons;
  curls
Wag or crossbridle, in a wind lifted, windlaced –
      See his wind- lilylocks -laced;
Churlsgrace, too, child of Amansstrength, how it hangs or hurls
Them – broad in bluff hide his frowning feet lashed! raced
With, along them, cragiron under and cold furls –
      With-a-fountain's shining-shot furls.

Gerard Manley Hopkins
(1844–1889)

The Steam Threshing-machine with the Straw-carrier

Flush with the pond the lurid furnace burn'd
At eve, while smoke and vapour fill'd the yard;
The gloomy winter sky was dimly starr'd,
The fly-wheel with a mellow murmur turn'd;
While, ever rising on its mystic stair
In the dim light, from secret chambers borne,
The straw of harvest, sever'd from the corn,
Climb'd, and fell over, in the murky air.
I thought of mind and matter, will and law,
And then of him, who set his stately seal
Of Roman words on all the forms he saw
Of old-world husbandry; *I* could but feel
With what a rich precision *he* would draw
The endless ladder, and the booming wheel!

Charles Tennyson Turner
(1808–1879)

Auction

from: *The Sale at the Farm*

I trust the worst is over with this sale.
The old place had a strange look in the crowd:
The jostling and the staring and the creak
Of shuffled feet, the public laugh sent round,
The hammer's clink, the flippant auctioneer,
Number on number lengthening out the day:
Familiar things dishonoured, like old friends
Set up on high to scorning fools: and then
The ache of loss, and some dull sense that they
Would sell me last by parcels, till the dusk
Drew, in December sleet, and all were gone:
And this old wreck bowed at my drooping fire
In gathered shade unfriended and alone.
Bare walls and fixtures here: thus ends the tale.

George Barnes, the thriving farmer, warpt and shrunk
And naked to the bite of wind and wave.
On the blank threshold of his eightieth year,
Ripe for the parish union or the grave.
The man whose name was clean and word was sure,
Dishonoured: pattern farmer of the squire.
The farm of gapless hedge and pasture clean
Without a rush: I, broken, the safe man
As England's bank for credit? when old Groves,
Who never paid a punctual rent, scrapes on,
With his lean kine, like Egypt's plagues, at grass
Where sprouts one blade of herbage to the score
Of rushes stubbled close as urchin quills.

Lord De Tabley
(1835–1895)

Rural Evening

The whip cracks on the plough-team's flank,
    The thresher's flail beats duller.
The round of day has warmed a bank
    Of cloud to primrose colour.

The dairy girls cry home the kine,
    The kine in answer lowing;
And rough-haired louts with sleepy shouts
    Keep crows whence seed is growing.

The creaking wain, brushed through the lane
    Hangs straws on hedges narrow;
And smoothly cleaves the soughing plough,
    And harsher grinds the harrow.

Comes, from the road-side inn caught up,
    A brawl of crowded laughter,
Thro' falling brooks and cawing rooks
    And a fiddle scrambling after.

Lord De Tabley
(1835–1895)

An Autumn Wind

from: In Memoriam

To-night the winds begin to rise
    And roar from yonder dropping day:
    The last red leaf is whirl'd away,
The rooks are blown about the skies;

The forest crack'd, the waters curl'd,
    The cattle huddled on the lea;
    And wildly dash'd on tower and tree
The sunbeam strikes along the world:

And but for fancies, which aver
    That all thy motions gently pass
    Athwart a plane of molten glass,
I scarce could brook the strain and stir

That makes the barren branches loud;
    And but for fear it is not so,
    The wild unrest that lives in woe
Would dote and pore on yonder cloud

That rises upward always higher,
    And onward drags a labouring breast,
    And topples round the dreary west,
A looming bastion fringed with fire.

Alfred Lord Tennyson
(1809–1892)

Thatcher

Bespoke for weeks, he turned up some morning
Unexpectedly, his bicycle slung
With a light ladder and a bag of knives.
He eyed the old rigging, poked at the eaves,

Opened and handled sheaves of lashed wheat-straw.
Next, the bundled rods: hazel and willow
Were flicked for weight, twisted in case they'd snap.
It seemed he spent the morning warming up:

Then fixed the ladder, laid out well honed blades
And snipped at straw and sharpened ends of rods
That, bent in two, made a white-pronged staple
For pinning down his world, handful by handful.

Couchant for days on sods above the rafters
He shaved and flushed the butts, stitched all together
Into a sloped honeycomb, a stubble patch,
And left them gaping at his Midas touch.

Seamus Heaney
(1939—2013)

Throwing a Tree
New Forest

The two executioners stalk along over the knolls,
Bearing two axes with heavy heads shining and wide,
And a long limp two-handled saw toothed for cutting great boles,
And so they approach the proud tree that bears the death-mark
on its side.

Jackets doffed they swing axes and chop away just above ground,
And the chips fly about and lie white on the moss and fallen leaves;
Till a broad deep gash in the bark is hewn all the way round,
And one of them tries to hook upward a rope, which at last he achieves.

The saw then begins, till the top of the tall giant shivers:
The shivers are seen to grow greater each cut than before:
They edge out the saw, tug the rope; but the tree only quivers,
And kneeling and sawing again, they step back to try pulling once
more.

Then, lastly, the living mast sways, further sways: with a shout
Job and Ike rush aside. Reached the end of its long staying powers
The tree crashes downward: it shakes all its neighbours throughout,
And two hundred years' steady growth has been ended in less than
two hours.

Thomas Hardy
(1840–1928)

The Seasons

Kentish Spring

from: The Land

Then broke the spring. The hedges in a day
Burgeoned to green; the drawing of the trees,
Incomparably pencilled line by line,
Thickened to heaviness, and men forgot
The intellectual austerity
Of winter, in the rich warm-blood rush
Of growth, and mating beasts, and rising sap.
How swift and sudden strode that tardy spring,
Between a sunrise and a sunset come!
The shadow of a swallow crossed the wall;
Nightingales sang by day. The pushing blade
Parted the soil. The morning roofs and oasts
There, down the lane, beside the brook and willows,
Cast their long shadows. Pasture, ankle-wet,
Steamed to the sun. The tulips dyed their green
To red in cottage gardens. Bees astir,
Fussing from flower to flower, made war on time.
Body and blood were princes; the cold mind
Sank with Orion from the midnight sky;
The stars of spring rose visible: The Virgin;
Al Fard the solitary; Regulus

The kingly star, the handle of the Sickle;
And Venus, lonely splendour in the west,
Roamed over the rapt meadows; shone in gold
Beneath the cottage eaves where nesting birds
Obeyed love's law; shone through the cottage panes
Where youth lay sleeping on the breast of youth,
Where love was life, and not a brief desire;
Shone on the heifer blaring for the bull
Over the hedgerow deep in dewy grass:
And glinted through the dark and open door
Where the proud stallion neighing to his mares
Stamped on the cobbles of the stable floor.

Vita Sackville-West
(1892–1962)

April

from: Prologue to the Canterbury Tales

Whan that Aprille with his shoures sote
The droghte of Marche hath perced to the rote,
And bathed every veyne in swich licour,
Of which vertu engendred is the flour;
Whan Zephirus eek with his swete breeth
Inspired hath in every holt and heeth
The tendre croppes, and the yonge sonne
Hath in the Ram his halfe cours y-ronne,
And smale fowles maken melodye,
That slepen al the night with open yë,
(So priketh hem nature in hir corages):
Than longen folk to goon on pilgrimages.

Geoffrey Chaucer
(1340[?]–1400)

Nature and Man

from: Queen Mab

Look on yonder earth:
The golden harvests spring; the unfailing sun
Sheds light and life; the fruits, the flowers, the trees,
Arise in due succession; all things speak
Peace, harmony, and love. The universe,
In nature's silent eloquence, declares
That all fulfil the works of love and joy, –
All but the outcast man.

Percy Bysshe Shelley
(1792–1822)

Daybreak

from: *The Faithful Shepherdess*

See, the day begins to break,
And the light shoots like a streak
Of subtle fire; the wind blows cold,
Whilst the morning doth unfold;
Now the birds begin to rouse,
And the squirrel from the boughs
Leaps, to get him nuts and fruit:
The early lark, that erst was mute,
Carols to the rising day
Many a note and many a lay!

John Fletcher
(1579–1625)

Spring

from: Two Moods

This aged earth that each new spring
Comes forth so young, so ravishing
In summer robes for all to see,
Of flower, and leaf, and bloomy tree,
For all her scarlet, gold, and green,
Fails not to keep within unseen
That inner purpose and that force
Which on the untiring orbit's course
Around the sun, amidst the spheres
Still bears her thro' the eternal years.

Arthur Hugh Clough
(1819–1861)

Summer Rain

Thick lay the dust, uncomfortably white,
In glaring mimicry of Arab sands.
The woods and mountains slept in hazy light;
The meadows look'd athirst and tawny tann'd;
The little rills had left their channels bare,
With scarce a pool to witness what they were;
And the shrunk river gleam'd 'mid oozy stones,
That stared like any famish'd giant's bones.

Sudden the hills grew black, and hot as stove
The air beneath; it was a toil to be.
There was a growling as of angry Jove
Provoked by Juno's prying jealousy –
A flash – a crash – the firmament was split,
And down it came in drops – the smallest fit
To drown a bee in fox-glove bell conceal'd;
Joy fill'd the brook, and comfort cheer'd the field.

Hartley Coleridge
(1796–1849)

The Evening Comes

from: Bacchanalia

The evening comes, the field is still.
The tinkle of the thirsty rill,
Unheard all day, ascends again;
Deserted is the new-reap'd grain,
Silent the sheaves! the ringing wain,
The reaper's cry, the dog's alarms,
All housed within the sleeping farms!

The business of the day is done,
The last belated gleaner gone.
And from the thyme upon the height,
And from the elder-blossom white
And pale dog-roses in the hedge,
And from the mint-plant in the sedge,
In puffs of balm the night-air blows
The perfume which the day forgoes.
And on the pure horizon far,
See, pulsing with the first-born star,
The liquid sky above the hill!
The evening comes, the field is still.

Matthew Arnold
(1822–1888)

On a Lane in Spring

A little lane – the brook runs close beside,
    And spangles in the sunshine, while the fish glide swiftly by;
And hedges leafing with the green springtide;
    From out their greenery the old birds fly,
And chirp and whistle in the morning sun;
    The pilewort glitters 'neath the pale blue sky,
The little robin has its nest begun
    The grass-green linnets round the bushes fly.
How mild the spring comes in! the daisy buds
    Lift up their golden blossoms to the sky.
How lovely are the pingles in the woods!
    Here a beetle runs – and there a fly
Rests on the arum leaf in bottle-green,
And all the spring in this sweet lane is seen.

John Clare
(1793–1864)

The Lichen on the Walls

Ah! the lichen on the walls
    Out in patches, white and red,
Where the creeping ivy crawls
    O'er the tree-stems overhead,
Is a token that no throng
Bustles by them all day long,
Ever wearing roadways bare
As they drive the whirling air
    Where the way
    Is not footless, night or day.

In the ever-busy street,
    Where we see no growing grass,
Streaming folk that briskly meet
    Throng each other as they pass;
Rubbing wall-sides to a gloss
Where is little soil for moss
That can seldom linger quick
On the ever-fretted brick,
    And no seed
    Ever quickens to a weed.

Here the words of fewer men
    Come with sounds of bird and bee,
And the mossy-nested wren
    Flits from ivy on the tree.
And the open sunshine glows
On the lily or the rose,
Leaving shaded air to cool
In the bower, and on the pool:
    And a sound
    Under others is not drown'd.

There are sire and wife, now old,
    And two sons, both hale and lithe;
And two maids of comely mould
    Who are ever kind and blithe.
And whenever maid and son
Shall have mated, one by one,
Then, as peaceful be the life
Of the husband and the wife,
    As they all
    Have within the garden wall.

William Barnes
(1801–1886)

The Wheat Field in Summer

from: The Farmer's Boy

Shot up from the broad rank blades that droop below,
The nodding Wheat-ear forms a graceful bow,
With milky kernels starting full, weigh'd down,
Ere yet the sun hath ting'd its head with brown;
There thousands in a flock, for ever gay,
Loud chirping sparrows welcome on the day,
And from the mazes of the leafy thorn
Drop one by one upon the bending corn.
Giles with a pole assails their close retreats,
And round the grass-grown dewy border beats,
On either side completely overspread,
Here branches bend, there corn o'ertops his head.
Green covert, hail! for through the varying year
No hours so sweet, no scene to him so dear.
Stretcht on the turf he lies, a peopled bed,
Where swarming insects creep around his head.
The small dust-colour'd beetle climbs with pain,
O'er the smooth plantain-leaf, a spacious plain!
Thence higher still, by countless steps convey'd,
He gains the summit of a shiv'ring blade,
And flirts his filmy wings, and looks around,
Exulting in his distance from the ground.
The tender speckled moth here dancing seen,
The vaulting grasshopper of glossy green,
And all prolific Summer's sporting train,
Their little lives by various pow'rs sustain.

Robert Bloomfield
(1766–1823)

Nightfall

from: The Seasons

Among the crooked lanes, on every hedge,
The Glow-worm lights his gem; and through the dark,
A moving radiance twinkles. Evening yields
The world to Night; not in her winter robe
Of massy Stygian woof, but loose array'd
In mantle dun. A faint erroneous ray,
Glanced from th' imperfect surfaces of things,
Flings half an image on the straining eye;
While wavering woods, and villages, and streams,
And rocks, and mountain-tops, that long retain'd,
Th' ascending gleam, are all one swimming scene,
Uncertain if beheld. Sudden to heaven
Thence weary vision turns; where, leading soft
The silent hours of love, with purest ray
Sweet Venus shines; and, from her genial rise,
When day-light sickens, till it springs afresh,
Unrivall'd reigns, the fairest lamp of night.
As thus th' effulgence tremulous I drink
With cherish'd gaze, the lambent lightnings shoot
Across the sky, or horizontal dart
In wondrous shapes, by fearful murmuring crowds
Portentous deem'd. Amid the radiant orbs,
That more than deck – that animate – the sky,
The life-infusing suns of other worlds;
Lo! from the dread immensity of space
Returning, with accelerated course,
The rushing comet to the Sun descends;
And as he sinks below the shading earth,
With awful train projected o'er the heavens,
The guilty nations tremble....

James Thomson
(1700–1748)

Oxfordshire

from: The Scholar Gipsy

And, above Godstow Bridge, when hay-time's here
In June, and many a scythe in sunshine flames,
Men who through those wide fields of breezy grass
Where black-wing'd swallows haunt the glittering Thames,
To bathe in the abandon'd lasher pass,
Have often pass'd thee near
Sitting upon the river bank o'ergrown:
Mark'd thy outlandish garb, thy figure spare,
Thy dark vague eyes, and soft abstracted air;
But, when they came from bathing, thou wert gone.

At some lone homested in the Cumnor hills,
Where at her open door the housewife darns,
Thou has been seen, or hanging on a gate
To watch the threshers in the mossy barns.
Children, who early range these slopes and late
For cresses from the rills,
Have known thee watching, all an April day,
The springing pastures and the feeding kine;
And mark'd thee, when the stars come out and shine,
Through the long dewy grass move slow away.

In Autumn, on the skirts of Bagley wood,
Where most the Gipsies by the turf-edg'd way
Pitch their smok'd tents, and every bush you see
With scarlet patches tagg'd and shreds of grey,
Above the forest ground call'd Thessaly –
The blackbird picking food
Sees thee, nor stops his meal, nor fears at all;
So often has he known thee past him stray
Rapt, twirling in thy hand a wither'd spray,
And waiting for the spark from Heaven to fall.

Matthew Arnold
(1822–1888)

Home Pictures in May

The sunshine bathes in clouds of many hues
And morning's feet are gemmed with early dews,
Warm daffodils about the garden beds
Peep through their pale slim leaves their golden heads,
Sweet earthly nuns of Spring; the gosling broods
In coats of sunny green about the road
Waddle in extasy; and in rich moods
The old hen leads her flickering chicks abroad,
Oft scuttling 'neath her wings to see the kite
Hang wavering o'er them in the spring's blue light.
The sparrows round their new nests chirp with glee
And sweet the robin Spring's young luxury shares
Tootling its song in feathery gooseberry tree
While watching worms the gardener's spade unbares.

John Clare
(1793–1864)

Summer Shower

A drop fell on the apple tree,
Another on the roof;
A half a dozen kissed the eaves,
And made the gables laugh.

A few went out to help the brook,
That went to help the sea.
Myself conjectured, Were they pearls,
What necklaces could be!

The dust replaced in hoisted roads,
The birds jocoser sung;
The sunshine threw his hat away,

The orchards spangles hung.
The breezes brought dejected lutes,
And bathed them in the glee;
The East put out a single flag,
And signed the fête away.

Emily Dickinson
(1830–1886)

A Thunder Shower

And now a cloud, bright, huge and calm,
Rose, doubtful if for bale or balm;
O'ertoppling crags, portentous towers
Appear'd, at beck of viewless powers,
Along a rifted mountain range.
Untraceable and swift in change,
Those glittering peaks, disrupted, spread
To solemn bulks, seen overhead;
The sunshine quench'd, from one dark form
Fumed the appalling light of storm.
Straight to the zenith, black with bale,
The Gipsies' smoke rose deadly pale;
And one wide night of hopeless hue
Hid from the heart the recent blue.
And soon, with thunder crackling loud,
A flash within the formless cloud
Show'd vague recess, projection dim,
Line sailing rack, and shadowy rim,
Against the whirl of leaves and dust
Kine dropp'd their heads; the tortured gust
Jagg'd and convuls'd the ascending smoke

To mockery of the lightning's stroke.
The blood prick'd, and a blinding flash
And close co-instantaneous crash
Humbled the soul, and the rain all round
Resilient dimm'd the whistling ground,
Nor flagged in force from first to last,
Till, sudden as it came, 'twas past,
Leaving a trouble in the copse
Of brawling birds and tinkling drops.

    Change beyond hope! Far thunder faint
Mutter'd its vast and vain complaint,
And gaps and fractures, fringed with light,
Show'd the sweet skies, with squadrons bright
Of cloudlets, glittering calm and fair
Through gulfs of calm and glittering air.

Coventry Patmore
(1823–1896)

On a Wet Summer

All ye, who far from town, in rural hall,
Like me, were wont to dwell near pleasant field,
Enjoying all the sunny day did yield,
With me the change lament, in irksome thrall,
By rains incessant held; for now no call
From early swain invites my hand to wield
The scythe; in parlour dim I sit concealed,
And mark the lessening sand from hour-glass fall;
Or 'neath my window view the wistful train
Of dripping poultry, whom the vine's broad leaves
Shelter no more. – Mute is the mournful plain,
Silent the swallow sits beneath the thatch,
And vacant hind hangs pensive o'er his hatch,
Counting the frequent drop from reeded eaves.

John Bampfylde
(1754–1796)

Young Lambs

The spring is coming by a many signs;
    The trays are up, the hedges broken down,
That fenced the haystack, and the remnant shines
    Like some old antique fragment weathered brown.
And where suns peep, in every sheltered place,
    The little early buttercups unfold
A glittering star or two – till many trace
    The edges of the blackthorn clumps in gold.
And then a little lamb bolts up behind
    The hill and wags his tail to meet the yoe,
And then another, sheltered from the wind,
    Lies all his length as dead – and lets me go
Close bye and never stirs but baking lies,
    With legs stretched out as though he could not rise.

John Clare
(1793–1864)

Autumn and Winter

from: A Song to David

The cheerful holly, pensive yew,
And holy thorn, their trim renew;
　　　　The squirrel hoards his nuts:
All creatures batten o'er their stores,
And careful nature all her doors
　　　　For ADORATION shuts.

* * * * * * *

The laurels with the winter strive;
The crocus burnishes alive
　　　　Upon the snow-clad earth.
For ADORATION myrtles stay
To keep the garden from dismay,
　　　　And bless the sight from dearth.

Christopher Smart
(1722–1771)

Storm and Sunlight

I

In barns we crouch, and under stacks of straw,
Harking the storm that rides a hurtling legion
Up the arched sky, and speeds quick heels of panic
With growling thunder loosed in fork and clap
That echoes crashing thro' the slumbrous vault.
> The whispering woodlands darken: vulture Gloom
> Stoops, menacing the skeltering flocks of Light,
> Where the gaunt shepherd shakes his gleaming staff
> And foots with angry tidings down the slope.
Drip, drip; the rain steals in through soaking thatch
By cob-webbed rafters to the dusty floor.
Drums shatter in the tumult; wrathful Chaos
Points pealing din to the zenith, then resolves
Terror in wonderment with rich collapse.

II

Now from drenched eaves a swallow darts to skim
The crystal stillness of an air unveiled
To tremulous blue. Raise your bowed heads, and let
Your horns adore the sky, ye patient kine!
Haste, flashing brooks! Small, chuckling rills, rejoice!
Be open-eyed for Heaven, ye pools of peace!
Shine, rain-bow hills! Dream on, fair glimpséd vale
In haze of drifting gold! And all sweet birds,
Sing out your raptures to the radiant leaves!
And ye, close huddling Men, come forth to stand
A moment simple in the gaze of God
That sweeps along your pastures! Breathe his might!
Lift your blind faces to be filled with day,
And share his benediction with the flowers.

Siegfried Sassoon
(1886–1967)

Winter

The boughs, the boughs are bare enough
But earth has never felt the snow.
Frost-furred our ivies are, and rough

With bills of rime the brambles shew.
The hoarse leaves crawl on hissing ground
Because the sighing wind is low.

But if the rain-blasts be unbound
And from dank feathers wring the drops
The clogged brook runs with choking sound

Kneading the mounded mire that stops
His channel under damming coats
Of foliage fallen in the copse.

A simple passage of weak notes
Is all the winter bird dare try
The bugle moon by daylight floats

So glassy white about the sky,
So like a berg of hyaline,
And pencilled blue so daintily,

I never saw her so divine
But through black branches, rarely drest
In scarves of silky shot and shine.

The webbèd and the watery west
Where yonder crimson fireball sits
Looks laid for feasting and for rest.

I see long reefs of violets
In beryl-covered fens so dim,
A gold-water Pactolus frets

Its brindled wharves and yellow brim,
The waxen colours weep and run
And slendering to his burning rim

Into the flat blue mist the sun
Drops out and all our day is done.

Gerard Manley Hopkins
(1844–1889)

A Winter Night

It was a chilly winter's night;
   And frost was glitt'ring on the ground,
And evening stars were twinkling bright;
   And from the gloomy plain around
      Came no sound,
But where, within the wood-girt tow'r,
The churchbell slowly struck the hour;

As if that all of human birth
   Had risen to the final day,
And soaring from the wornout earth
   Were called in hurry and dismay,
      Far away;
And I alone of all mankind
Were left in loneliness behind.

William Barnes
(1801–1886)

Birds at Winter Nightfall

Around the house the flakes fly faster,
And all the berries now are gone
From holly and cotoneaster
Around the house. The flakes fly! faster
Shutting indoors that crumb-outcaster
We used to see upon the lawn
Around the house. The flakes fly faster,
And all the berries now are gone!

Thomas Hardy
(1840–1928)

Snow Storm

What a night! The wind howls, hisses, and but stops
To howl more loud, while the snow volley keeps
Incessant batter at the window pane,
Making our comfort feel as sweet again;
And in the morning, when the tempest drops,
At every cottage door mountainous heaps
Of snow lie drifted, that all entrance stops
Until the beesom and the shovel gain
The path, and leave a wall on either side.
The shepherd rambling valleys white and wide
With new sensations his old memory fills,
When hedges left at night, no more descried,
Are turned to one white sweep of curving hills,
And trees turned bushes half their bodies hide.

The boy that goes to fodder with surprise
Walks oer the gate he opened yesternight.
The hedges all have vanished from his eyes;
Een some tree tops the sheep could reach to bite.
The novel scene emboldens new delight,
And, though with cautious steps his sports begin,
He bolder shuffles the huge hills of snow,
Till down he drops and plunges to the chin,
And struggles much and oft escape to win –
Then turns and laughs but dare not further go;
For deep the grass and bushes lie below,
Where little birds that soon at eve went in
With heads tucked in their wings now pine for day
And little feel boys oer their heads can stray.

John Clare
(1793–1864)

A Frosty Day

Grass afield wears silver thatch;
    Palings all are edged with rime;
Frost-flowers pattern round the latch;
    Cloud nor breeze dissolve the clime;

When the waves are solid floor,
    And the clods are iron-bound,
And the boughs are crystall'd hoar,
    And the red leaf nailed a-ground.

When the fieldfare's flight is slow,
    And a rosy vapour rim,
Now the sun is small and low,
    Belts along the region dim.

When the ice-crack flies and flaws,
    Shore to shore, with thunder shock,
Deeper than the evening daws,
    Clearer than the village clock.

When the rusty blackbird strips,
    Bunch by bunch, the coral thorn;
And the pale day-crescent dips,
    Now to heaven, a slender horn.

Lord De Tabley
(1835–1895)

A Wet Winter

from: A Midsummer Night's Dream

Therefore the winds, piping to us in vain,
As in revenge have sucked up from the sea
Contagious fogs: which, falling in the land,
Hath every pelting river made so proud
That they have overborne their continents.
The ox hath therefore stretched his yoke in vain,
The ploughman lost his sweat, and the green corn
Hath rotted ere his youth attained a beard.
The fold stands empty in the drownèd field,
And crows are fatted with the murrion flock,
The nine men's morris is filled up with mud,
And the quaint mazes in the wanton green
For lack of tread are undistinguishable.

William Shakespeare
(1564–1616)

Thunder Storm

from: The Seasons

A boding Silence reigns,
Dread thro the dun Expanse; save the dull Sound
That from the Mountain, previous to the Storm,
Rolls o'er the muttering Earth, disturbs the Flood,
And shakes the Forest-Leaf without a Breath.
Prone, to the lowest Vale, the aërial Tribes
Descend; the Tempest-loving Raven scarce
Dares wing the dubious Dusk. In rueful Gaze
The Cattle stand, and on the scouling Heavens
Cast a deploring Eye; by Man forsook,
Who to the crouded Cottage hies him fast,
Or seeks the Shelter of the downward Cave.

'Tis listening Fear, and dumb Amazement all:
When to the startled Eye the sudden Glance
Appears far South, eruptive thro the Cloud;
And following slower, in Explosion vast,
The Thunder raises his temendous voice.
At first, heard solemn o'er the Verge of Heaven,
The Tempest growls; but as it nearer comes,
And rolls its awful Burden on the Wind,
The Lightnings flash a larger Curve, and more
The Noise astounds: till over Head a Sheet
Of livid Flame, discloses wide, then shuts
And opens wider, shuts and opens still
Expansive, wrapping Ether in a Blaze.
Follows the loosen'd aggravated Roar,
Enlarging, deepening, mingling, Peal on Peal
Crush'd horrible, convulsing Heaven and Earth.

Down comes a Deluge of sonorous Hail,
Or prone-descending Rain. Wide-rent, the Clouds
Pour a whole Flood; and yet, its Flame unquench'd,
Th' unconquerable Lightning struggles thro,
Ragged and fierce, or in red whirling Balls,
And fires the Mountains with redoubled Rage.
Black from the Stroke, above, the smould'ring Pine
Stands a sad shatter'd Trunk; and, stretch'd below,
A lifeless Groupe the blasted Cattle lie:
Here the soft Flocks, with that same harmlevvss Look
They wore alive, and ruminating still
In Fancy's Eye; and there the frowning Bull,
And Ox half-rais'd. Struck on the castled Cliff,
The venerable Tower and spiry Fane
Resign their aged Pride. The gloomy Woods
Start at the Flash, and from their deep Recess,
Wide-flaming out, their trembling Inmates shake.
Amid Carnarvon's Mountains rages loud
The repercussive Roar: with mighty Crush,
Into the flashing Deep, from the rude Rocks
Of Penmaen Maur heap'd hideous to the sky,
Tumble the smitten Cliffs; and Snowdon's Peak,
Dissolving, instant yields his wintry Load.
Far-seen, the Heights of heathy Cheviot blaze,
And Thulè bellows thro her utmost Isles.

As from the Face of Heaven the shatter'd Clouds
Tumultuous rove, th' interminable Sky
Sublimer swells, and o'er the World expands
A purer Azure. Nature, from the Storm,
Shines out afresh; and thro the lighten'd Air
A higher Luster and a clearer calm,
Diffusive, tremble, while as if in sign
Of Danger past, a glittering Robe of Joy,
Set off abundant by the yellow Ray,
Invests the fields, yet dropping from Distress.

James Thomson
(1700–1748)

At Midnight

from: The Complaint of Henry Stafford, Duke of Buckingham

Midnight was come, and every vital thing
With sweet sound sleep their weary limbs did rest,
The beasts were still, the little birds that sing,
Now sweetly slept beside their mother's breast,
The old and all well shrouded in their nest;
    The waters calm, the cruel seas did cease,
    The woods, the fields, and all things held their peace.

The golden stars were whirl'd amid their race,
And on the earth did with their twinkling light,
When each thing nestled in his resting-place,
Forget day's pain with pleasure of the night;
The hare had not the greedy hounds in sight,
    The fearful deer of death stood not in doubt,
    The partridge dreamt not of the falcon's foot.

Thomas Sackville, Lord Buckhurst
(1536–1608)

A Suffolk Landscape

from: The Borough

Thy walks are ever pleasant; every scene
Is rich in beauty, lively, or serene –
Rich – is that varied view with woods around,
Seen from the seat within the shrubb'ry bound;
Where shines the distant lake, and where appear
From ruins bolting, unmolested deer;
Lively – the village-green, the inn, the place,
Where the good widow schools her infant-race.
Shops, whence are heard the hammer and the saw,
And village-pleasures unreproved by law:
Then how serene! when in your favourite room,
Gales from your jasmines soothe the evening gloom;
When from your upland paddock you look down,
And just perceive the smoke which hides the town;
When weary peasants at the close of day
Walk to their cots, and part upon the way;
When cattle slowly cross the shallow brook,
And shepherds pen their folds, and rest upon their crook.
We prune our hedges, prime our slender trees,
And nothing looks untutor'd and at ease,
On the wide heath, or in the flow'ry vale,
We scent the vapours of the sea-born gale;
Broad-beaten paths lead on from stile to stile,
And sewers from streets the road-side banks defile;
Our guarded fields a sense of danger show,
Where garden-crops with corn and clover grow.

George Crabbe
(1754–1832)

A Wren's Nest

Among the dwellings framed by birds
    In field or forest with nice care,
Is none that with the little Wren's
    In snugness may compare.

No door the tenement requires,
    And seldom needs a laboured roof:
Yet is it to the fiercest sun
    Impervious, and storm-proof

So warm, so beautiful withal,
    In perfect fitness for its aim,
That to the Kind by special grace
    Their instinct surely came.

And when for their abodes they seek
    An opportune recess,
The hermit has no finer eye
    For shadowy quietness.

These find, 'mid ivied abbey-walls,
    A canopy in some still nook;
Others are pent-housed by a brae
    That overhangs a brook.

There to the brooding bird her mate
    Warbles by fits his low clear song;
And by the busy streamlet both
    Are sung to all day long.

Or in sequestered lanes they build,
    Where, till the flitting bird's return,
Her eggs within the nest repose,
    Like relics in an urn.

But still, where general choice is good,
    There is a better and a best;
And, among fairest objects, some
    Are fairer than the rest;

This, one of those small builders proved
    In a green covert, where, from out
The forehead of a pollard oak,
    The leafy antlers sprout;

For She who planned the mossy lodge,
    Mistrusting her evasive skill,
Had to a Primrose looked for aid
    Her wishes to fulfil.

High on the trunk's projecting brow,
    And fixed an infant's span above
The budding flowers, peeped forth the nest
    The prettiest of the grove!

The treasure proudly did I show
    To some whose minds without disdain
Can turn to little things; but once
    Looked up for it in vain:

'Tis gone – a ruthless spoiler's prey,
    Who heeds not beauty, love, or song,
'Tis gone! (so seemed it) and we grieved
    Indignant at the wrong.

Just three days after, passing by
    In clearer light and moss-built cell
I saw, espied its shaded mouth;
    And felt that all was well.

The Primrose for a veil had spread
  The largest of her upright leaves;
And thus, for purposes benign,
  A simple flower deceives.

Concealed from friends who might disturb
  Thy quiet with no ill intent,
Secure from evil eyes and hands
  On barbarous plunder bent,

Rest, Mother-bird! and when thy young
  Take flight, and thou art free to roam,
When withered is the guardian Flower,
  And empty thy late home,

Think how ye prospered, thou and thine,
  Amid the unviolated grove,
Housed near the growing Primrose-tuft
  In foresight, or in love.

William Wordsworth
(1770–1850)

Still Evening

from: Paradise Lost

Now came still Evening on, and Twilight grey
Had in her sober livery all things clad;
Silence accompanied; for beast and bird,
They to their grassy couch, these to their nests
Were slunk, all but the wakeful nightingale;
She all night long her amorous descant sung:
Silence was pleased. Now glowed the firmament
With living sapphires; Hesperus, that led
The starry host, rode brightest, till the Moon,
Rising in clouded majesty, at length
Apparent queen, unveiled her peerless light,
And o'er the dark her silver mantle threw.

John Milton
(1608–1674)

Birds and Beasts

Grasshopper

from: *The Grasshopper*

Oh thou that swing'st upon the waving eare
    Of some well-filled Oaten Beard,
Drunke ev'ry night with a Delicious teare
    Dropt thee from Heav'n, where now th'art reard.

The Joyes of Earth and Ayre are thine in tire,
    That with thy feet and wings dost hop and flye;
And when thy Poppy workes thou dost retire
    To thy Carv'd Acorn-bed to lye.

Up with the Day, the Sun thou welcomst then,
    Sportst in the guilt-plats of his Beames,
And all these merry dayes mak'st merry men,
    Thy selfe, and Melancholy streames.

But ah the Sickle! Golden Eares are Cropt;
    Ceres and Bacchus bid goodnight;
Sharpe frosty fingers all your Flowr's have topt,
    And what scithes spar'd, Winds shave off quite.

Poore verdant foole! and now green Ice! thy Joys
    Large and as lasting as thy Porch of Grasse,
Bid us lay in 'gainst Winter, Raine, and poize
    Their flouds, with an o'erflowing glasse . . .

Richard Lovelace
(1618–1658)

The Study of a Spider

From holy flower to holy flower
Thou weavest thine unhallowed bower.
The harmless dewdrops, beaded thin,
Ripple along thy ropes of sin.
Thy house a grave, a gulf thy throne
Affright the fairies every one.
Thy winding sheets are grey and fell,
Imprisoning with nets of hell
The lovely births that winnow by,
Winged sisters of the rainbow sky:
Elf-darlings, fluffy, bee-bright things,
And owl-white moths with mealy wings,
And tiny flies, as gauzy thin
As e'er were shut electrum in.
These are thy death spoils, insect ghoul,
With their dear life thy fangs are foul.
Thou felon anchorite of pain
Who sittest in a world of slain.
Hermit, who tunest song unsweet
To heaving wing and writhing feet.
A glutton of creation's sighs,
Miser of many miseries.
Toper, whose lonely feasting chair
Sways in inhospitable air.
The board is bare, the bloated host
Drinks to himself toast after toast.
His lip requires no goblet brink,
But like a weasel must he drink.
The vintage is as old as time
And bright as sunset, pressed and prime.

Ah, venom mouth and shaggy thighs
And paunch grown sleek with sacrifice,
Thy dolphin back and shoulders round
Coarse-hairy, as some goblin hound
Whom a hag rides to sabbath on,
While shuddering stars in fear grow wan.
Thou palace priest of treachery,
Thou type of selfish lechery,
I break the toils around thy head
And from their gibbets take thy dead.

Lord De Tabley
(1835–1895)

Sweet Suffolke Owle

Sweet Suffolke Owle, so trimly dight,
With feathers like a Lady bright,
Thou sing'st alone, sitting, by night,
      Te whit, te whoo,
Thy note that forth so freely roules,
With shrill command the Mouse controules,
And sings a dirge for dying soules,
      Te whit, te whoo.

Anonymous

Spring Song

About the flowerless land adventurous bees
    Pickeering hum; the rooks debate, divide,
    With many a hoarse aside,
In solemn conclave on the budding trees;
Larks in the skies and plough-boys o'er the leas
Carol as if the winter never had been;
    The very owl comes out to greet the sun;
    Rivers high-hearted run;
And hedges mantle with a flush of green.

The curlew calls me where the salt winds blow;
    His troubled note dwells mournfully and dies;
    Then the long echo cries
Deep in my heart. Ah, surely I must go!
For there the tides, moon-haunted, ebb and flow;
And there the seaboard murmurs resonant;
    The waves their interwoven fugue repeat
    And brooding surges beat
A slow, melodious, continual chant.

John Davidson
(1857–1909)

The Birds of the Fens

from: Poly-Olbion

The diving Dob-chick, here among the rest you see,
Now up, now downe againe, that hard it is to proove,
Whether under water most it liveth, or above:
With which last little fowle, (that water may not lacke;
More then the Dob-chick doth, and more doth love the brack)
The Puffin we compare, which comming to the dish,
Nice pallats hardly judge, if it be flesh or fish.
　　But wherefore should I stand upon such toyes as these,
That have so goodly fowles, the wandring eye to please.
Here in my vaster pooles, as white as snow or milke,
(In water blacke as Stix) swimmes the wild Swanne, the Ilke,
Of Hollanders so tearm'd, no niggard of his breath
(As poets say of Swannes, which onely sing in death)
But oft as other birds, is heard his tunes to roat,
Which like a trumpet comes, from his long arched throat,
And tow'rds this watry kind, about the flashes brimme,
Some cloven-footed are, by nature not to swimme.
There stalks the stately Crane, as though he march'd in warre,
By him that hath the Herne, which (by the fishy carre)
Can fetch with their long necks, out of the rush and reed,
Snigs, fry, and yellow frogs, whereon they often feed:
And under them againe, (that water never take,
But by some ditches side, or little shallow lake

Lye dabling night and day) the pallat-pleasing Snite,
The Bidcocke, and like them the Redshanke, that delight
Together still to be, in some small reedy bed,
In which these little fowles in summer time were bred.
The buzzing Bitter sits, which through his hollow bill,
A sudden bellowing sends, which many times doth fill
The neighbouring marsh with noyse, as though a bull did roare
But scarcely have I yet recited halfe my store:
And with my wondrous flocks of Wild-geese come I then,
Which looke as though alone they peopled all the fen,
Which here in winter time, when all is overflow'd,
And want of sollid sward inforceth them abroad,
Th'abundance then is seene, that my full fennes doe yeeld,
That almost through the isle, doe pester every field.
The Barnacles with them, which wheresoere they breed,
On trees, or rótten ships, yet to my fennes for feed
Continually they come, and chiefe abode doe make,
And very hardly forc'd my plenty to forsake:
Who almost all this kind doe challenge as mine owne,
Whose like I dare averre, is elsewhere hardly knowne.
For sure unlesse in me, no one yet ever saw
The multitudes of fowle, in mooting time they draw:
From which to many a one, much profit doth accrue.

Now such as flying feed, next these I must pursue;
The Sea-meaw, Sea-pye, Gull, and Curlew heere doe keepe,
As searching every shole, and watching every deepe.
To find the floating fry, with their sharpe-pearcing sight,
Which suddenly they take, by stouping from their height.
The Cormorant then comes, (by his devouring kind)
Which flying o're the fen, imediatly doth find
The fleet best stor'd of fish, when from his wings at full
As though he shot himselfe into the thickned skull,
He under water goes, and so the shoale pursues,
Which into creeks doe flie, when quickly he doth chuse,
The fin that likes him best, and rising, flying feeds.
The Ospray oft here seene, though seldome here it breeds,
Which over them the fish no sooner doe espie,
But (betwixt him and them, by an antipathy)
Turning their bellies up, as though their death they saw,
They at his pleasure lye, to stuffe his glutt'nous maw.

Michael Drayton
(1563–1631)

The Sweet o' the Year

Now the frog, all lean and weak,
    Yawning from his famished sleep,
Water in the ditch doth seek,
    Fast as he can stretch and leap:
        Marshy king-cups burning near
        Tell him 'tis the sweet o' the year.

Now the ant works up his mound
    In the mouldered piny soil,
And above the busy ground
    Takes the joy of earnest toil:
        Dropping pine-cones, dry and sere,
        Warn him 'tis the sweet o' the year.

Now the chrysalis on the wall
    Cracks, and out the creature springs,
Raptures in his body small,
    Wonders on his dusty wings:
        Bells and cups, all shining clear,
        Show him 'tis the sweet o' the year.

Now the brown bee, wild and wise,
    Hums abroad, and roves and roams,
Storing in his wealthy thighs
    Treasure for the golden combs:
        Dewy buds and blossoms dear
        Whisper 'tis the sweet o' the year.

Now the merry maids so fair
    Weave the wreaths and choose the queen,
Blooming in the open air,
    Like fresh flowers upon the green;
        Spring, in every thought sincere,
        Thrills them with the sweet o' the year.

Now the lads, all quick and gay,
　　Whistle to the browsing herds,
Or in the twilight pastures grey
　　Learn the use of whispered words:
　　　　First a blush, and then a tear,
　　　　And then a smile, i' the sweet o' the year.

Now the May-fly and the fish
　　Play again from noon to night;
Every breeze begets a wish,
　　Every motion means delight:
　　　　Heaven high over heath and mere
　　　　Crowns with blue the sweet o' the year.

Now all Nature is alive,
　　Bird and beetle, man and mole;
Bee-like goes the human hive,
　　Lark-like sings the soaring soul:
　　　　Hearty faith and honest cheer
　　　　Welcome in the sweet o' the year.

George Meredith
(1828–1909)

'I Watched a Blackbird'

I watched a blackbird on a budding sycamore
One Easter Day, when sap was stirring twigs to the core;
   I saw his tongue, and crocus-coloured bill
   Parting and closing as he turned his trill;
   Then he flew down, seized on a stem of hay,
And upped to where his building scheme was under way,
As if so sure a nest were never shaped on spray.

Thomas Hardy
(1840–1928)

The Robin

Poore bird! I doe not envie thee;
Pleas'd in the gentle Melodie
    Of thy owne Song.
Let crabbed winter Silence all
The winged Quire; he never shall
    Chaine up thy Tongue:
            Poore Innocent!
When I would please my selfe, I looke on thee;
And guess some sparkes of that Felicitie,
            That Selfe-Content.

When the bleake Face of winter Spreads
The Earth, and violates the Meads
    Of all their Pride;
When Sapless Trees and Flowere are fled,
Back to their Causes, and lye dead
    To all beside:
            I see thee Set,
Bidding defiance to the bitter Ayre,
Upon a wither'd Spray; by cold made bare.
            And drooping yet.

There, full in notes, to ravish all
My Earth, I wonder what to call
    My dullness; when
I heare thee, prettie Creature, bring
Thy better odes of Praise, and Sing,
    To puzzle men:
                Poore pious Elfe!
I am instructed by thy harmonie,
To sing the Time's uncertaintie,
                Safe in my Selfe.

Poore Redbreast, caroll out thy Laye,
And teach us mortalls what to saye.
    Here cease the Quire
Of ayerie Choristers; noe more
Mingle your notes; but catch a Store
    From her Sweet Lire;
                You are but weake,
Mere summer Chanters; you have neither wing
Nor voice, in winter. Prettie Redbreast, Sing,
                What I would speake.

George Daniel
(1562–1619)

The Darkling Thrush

I learnt upon a coppice gate
    When Frost was spectre-gray
And Winter's dregs made desolate
    The weakening eye of day.
The tangled bine-stems scored the sky
    Like strings of broken lyres,
And all mankind that haunted nigh
    Had sought their household fires.

The land's sharp features seemed to be
    The Century's corpse outleant,
His crypt the cloudy canopy,
    The wind his death-lament.
The ancient pulse of germ and birth
    Was shrunken hard and dry,
And every spirit upon earth
    Seemed fervourless as I.

At once a voice arose among
    The bleak twigs overhead
In a full-hearted evensong
    Of joy illimited;
An aged thrush, frail, gaunt, and small,
    In blast-beruffled plume,
Had chosen thus to fling his soul
    Upon the growing gloom.

So little cause for carolings
    Of such ecstatic sound
Was written on terrestial things
    Afar or nigh around,
That I could think there trembled through
    His happy good-night air
Some blessed Hope, whereof he knew
    And I was unaware.

Thomas Hardy
(1840–1928)

Dyke's Side

The frog croaks loud, and maidens dare not pass
But fear the noisome toad and shun the grass;
And on the sunny banks they dare not go
Where hissing snakes run to the flood below.
The nuthatch noises loud in wood and wild,
Like women turning skreeking to a child.
The schoolboy hears and brushes through the trees
And runs about till drabbled to the knees.
The old hawk winnows round the old crow's nest;
The schoolboy hears and wonder fills his breast.
He throws his basket down to climb the tree
And wonders what the red blotched eggs can be:
The green woodpecker bounces from the view
And hollos as he buzzes bye 'kew kew'

John Clare
(1793–1864)

The Lambs of Grasmere

The upland flocks grew starved and thinned:
    Their shepherds scarce could feed the lambs
Whose milkless mothers butted them,
    Or who were orphaned of their dams.
The lambs athirst for mother's milk
    Filled all the place with piteous sounds:
Their mothers' bones made white for miles
    The pastureless wet pasture grounds.

Day after day, night after night,
    From lamb to lamb the shepherds went,
With teapots for the bleating mouths,
    Instead of nature's nourishment.
The little shivering gaping things
    Soon knew the step that brought them aid,
And fondled the protecting hand,
    And rubbed it with a woolly head.

Then, as the days waxed on to weeks,
    It was a pretty sight to see
These lambs with frisky heads and tails
    Skipping and leaping on the lea,
Bleating in tender trustful tones,
    Resting on rocky crag or mound,
And following the beloved feet
    That once had sought for them and found.

These very shepherds of their flocks,
    These loving lambs so meek to please,
Are worthy of recording words
    And honour in their due degrees:
So I might live a hundred years,
    And roam from strand to foreign strand,
Yet not forget this flooded spring
    And scarce-saved lambs of Westmoreland.

Christina Rossetti
(1830–1894)

The Charming of the East Wind

Late in the month a rough east wind had sway,
The old trees thunder'd, and the dust was blown;
But other powers possess'd the night and day,
And soon he found he could not hold his own;
The merry ruddock whistled at his heart,
And strenuous blackbirds pierced his flanks with song,
Pert sparrows wrangled o'er his every part,
And through him shot the larks on pinions strong:
Anon a sunbeam broke across the plain,
And the wild bee went forth on booming wing –
Whereat he feeble wax'd, but rose again
With aimless rage, and idle blustering;
The south wind touch'd him with a drift of rain,
And down he sank, a captive to the spring!

Charles Tennyson Turner
(1808–1879)

On the Lancashire Coast

The rocks crawl down the beach,
Taking a thousand years to move a yard;
The sea-weed clogs their flippers; each
(Blind, dumb and yet gregarious) lifts an ear,
Like a bat's ear that measures space by echoes,
To catch the effervescence of the sea
Against a neighbour's ribs and shoulders.
Beside such boulders human life
Seems shorter than the suds of foam
Burst by blowing sand:
And yet these fingers (five
New to the touch of five) that bend
One to another like a lip
To speak a kiss, these hands
Shaping the deaf-mute language of the heart,
These wrists that time will strip
Quicker than it smooths the wrinkles on the stones,
Live with a vertical bright permanence
That cuts through death like a knife.

Norman Nicholson
(1914–1987)

The Lark Ascending

from: The Lark

He rises and begins to round,
He drops the silver chain of sound,
Of many links without a break,
In chirrup, whistle, slur and shake,
All intervolved and spreading wide,
Like water-dimples down a tide
Where ripple ripple overcurls
And eddy into eddy whirls;
A press of hurried notes that run
So fleet they scarce are more than one,
Yet changeingly the trills repeat
And linger ringing while they fleet,
Sweet to the quick o' the ear, and dear
To her beyond the handmaid ear,
Who sits beside our inner springs,
Too often dry for this he brings,
Which seems the very jet of earth
At sight of sun, her music's mirth,
As up he winds the spiral stair,
A song of light, and pierces air
With fountain ardour, fountain play,
To reach the shining tops of day,
And drink in everything discerned
An ecstasy to music turned,
Impelled by what his happy bill
Disperses; drinking, showering still,
Unthinking save that he may give
His voice the outlet, there to live
Renewed in endless notes of glee,

So thirsty of his voice is he,
For all to hear and all to know
That he is joy, awake, aglow,
The tumult of the heart to hear
Through pureness filtered crystal-clear,
And know the pleasure sprinkled bright
By simple singing of delight,
Shrill, irreflective, unrestrained,
Rapt, ringing, on the jet sustained,
Without a break, without a fall,
Sweet silvery, sheer lyrical,
Perennial, quavering up the chord
Like myriad dews of sunny sward
That trembling into fulness shine,
And sparkle dropping argentine.

George Meredith
(1828–1909)

On a Summer's Morn

I love to peep out on a summer's morn,
    Just as the scouting rabbit seeks her shed,
And the coy hare squats nestling in the corn,
    Frit at the bow'd ear tott'ring o'er her head;
And blund'ring pheasant, that from covert springs,
    His short sleep broke by early trampling feet,
Makes one to startle with his rustling wings,
    As through the boughs he seeks more safe retreat.
The little flower, begemm'd around with drops
    That shine at sunrise like to burnish'd gold,
'Tis sweet to view: the milkmaid often stops,
    And wonders much such spangles to behold;
The hedger, too, admires them deck the thorn, –
    And thinks he sees no beauties like the Morn.

John Clare
(1793–1864)

At Sunset

The shadows now so long do grow
That brambles like tall cedars grow;
Molehills seem mountains, and the ant
Appears a monstrous elephant.
A very little, little flock
Shades thrice the ground that it would stock,
Whilst the small stripling following them
Appears a mighty Polytheme.

Charles Cotton
(1630–1687)

Landscapes
and
Seascapes

The Herefordshire Landscape

from: Aurora Leigh

I dared to rest, or wander, – like a rest
Made sweeter for the step upon the grass, –
And view the ground's most gentle dimplement,
(As if God's finger touched but did not press
In making England!) such an up and down
Of verdure, – nothing too much up or down
A ripple of land; such little hills, the sky
Can stoop to tenderly and the wheatfields climb;
Such nooks of valleys, lined with orchises,
Fed full of noises by invisible streams;
And open pastures, where you scarcely tell
White daisies from white dew, – at intervals
The mythic oaks and elm-trees standing out
Self-poised upon their prodigy of shade, –
I thought my father's land was worthy too
Of being my Shakespeare's...

                    Then the thrushes sang,
And shook my pulses and the elms' new leaves...
I flattered all the beauteous country round,
As poets use; the skies, the clouds, the fields,
The happy violets hiding from the roads
The primroses run down to, carrying gold, –
The tangled hedgerows, where the cows push out
Impatient horns and tolerant churning mouths
'Twixt dripping ash-boughs, – hedgerows all alive
With birds and gnats and large white butterflies
Which look as if the May-flower had caught life
And palpitated forth upon the wind, –
Hills, vales, woods, netted in a silver mist,
Farm, granges, doubled up among the hills,
And cattle grazing in the watered vales,
And cottage-chimneys smoking from the woods,
And cottage-gardens smelling everywhere,
Confused with smell of orchards.

Elizabeth Barrett Browning
(1806–1861)

View from the top of Black Comb

This height a ministering angel might select:
For from the summit of Black Comb (dread name
Derived from clouds and storms!) the amplest range
Of unobstructed prospect may be seen
That British ground commands: – low dusky tracts,
Where Trent is nursed, far southward! Cambrian hills
To the southwest, a multitudinous show;
And, in a line of eyesight linked with these,
The hoary peaks of Scotland that give birth
To Tcviot's stream, to Annan, Tweed, and Clyde: –
Crowding the quarter whence the sun comes forth,
Gigantic mountains rough with crags; beneath,
Right at the imperial station's western base,
Main ocean, breaking audibly, and stretched
Far into silent regions blue and pale; –
And visibly engirding Mona's Isle,
That, as we left the plain, before our sight
Stood like a lofty mount, uplifting slowly
(Above the convex of the watery globe)
Into clear view the cultured fields that streak
Her habitable shores, but now appears
A dwindled object, and submits to lie
At the spectator's feet. – Yon azure ridge,
Is it a perishable cloud? or there
Do we behold the line of Erin's coast?
Land sometimes by the roving shepherd-swain
(Like the bright confines of another world)
Not doubtfully perceived. – Look homeward now!
In depth, in height, in circuit, how serene
The spectacle, how pure! – Of Nature's works,
In earth, and air, and earth-embracing sea,
A revelation infinite it seems;
Display august of man's inheritance,
Of Britain's calm felicity and power!

William Wordsworth
(1770–1850)

Woodland Scene

from: The Task

Nor less attractive is the woodland scene,
Diversified with trees of ev'ry growth,
Alike, yet various. Here the gray smooth trunks
Of ash, or lime, or beech, distinctly shine,
Within the twilight of their distant shades;
There, lost behind a rising ground, the wood
Seems sunk and shorten'd to its topmost boughs.
No tree in all the grove but has its charms,
Though each its hue peculiar; paler some,
And of a wannish gray; the willow such
And poplar, that with silver lines his leaf,
And ash far-stretching his umbrageous arm;
Of deeper green the elm; and deeper still,
Lord of the woods, the long-surviving oak.
Some glossy-leav'd, and shining in the sun,
The maple, and the beech of oily nuts
Prolific, and the lime at dewy eve
Diffusing odours: not unnoted pass
The sycamore, capricious in attire,
Now green, now tawny, and, ere autumn yet
Have chang'd the woods, in scarlet honours bright.
O'er these, but far beyond (a spacious map
Of hill and valley interpos'd between),
The Ouse, dividing the well-water'd land,
Now glitters in the sun, and now retires,
As bashful, yet impatient to be seen.

William Cowper
(1731–1800)

Binsey Poplars

(Felled 1879)

My aspens dear, whose airy cages quelled,
Quelled or quenched in leaves the leaping sun,
All felled, felled, are all felled;
    Of a fresh and following folded rank
          Not spared, not one
          That dandled a sandalled
   Shadow that swam or sank
On meadow and river and wind-wandering weed-winding bank.

O if we but knew what we do
   When we delve or hew –
Hack and rack the growing green!
   Since country is so tender
To touch, her being so slender,
That, like this sleek and seeing ball
But a prick will make no eye at all,
Where we, even where we mean
         To mend her we end her,
   When we hew or delve:
After-comers cannot guess the beauty been.
   Ten or twelve, only ten or twelve
    Strokes of havoc unselve
    The sweet especial scene,
Rural scene, a rural scene,
Sweet especial rural scene.

Gerard Manley Hopkins
(1844–1889)

A Brilliant Day

O keen pellucid air! nothing can lurk
Or disavow itself on this bright day;
The small rain-plashes shine from far away,
The tiny emmet glitters at his work;
The bee looks blithe and gay, and as she plies
Her task, and moves and sidles round the cup
Of this spring flower, to drink its honey up,
Her glassy wings, like oars that dip and rise,
Gleam momently. Pure-bosom'd, clear of fog,
The long lake glistens, while the glorious beam
Bespangles the wet joints and floating leaves
Of water-plants, whose every point receives
His light; and jellies of the spawning frog,
Unmark'd before, like piles of jewels seem!

Charles Tennyson Turner
(1808–1879)

Cambridgeshire

The stacks, like blunt impassive temples, rise
Across flat fields against the autumnal skies.
The hairy-footed horses plough the land,
Or as in prayer and meditation stand
Upholding square, primeval, dung-stained carts,
With an unending patience in their hearts.

Nothing is changed. The farmer's gig goes by
Against the horizon. Surely, the same sky,
So vast and yet familiar, grey and mild,
And streaked with light like music, I, a child,
Lifted my face from leaf-edged lanes to sec,
Late-coming home, to bread-and-butter tea.

Frances Cornford
(1886–1960)

Winter Seascape

The sea runs back against itself
    With scarcely time for breaking wave
To cannonade a slatey shelf
    And thunder under in a cave

Before the next can fully burst,
    The headwind, blowing harder still,
Smooths it to what it was at first –
    A slowly rolling water hill.

Against the breeze the breakers haste,
    Against the tide their ridges run
And all the sea's a dappled waste
    Criss-crossing underneath the sun.

Far down the beach the ripples drag
    Blown backward, rearing from the shore,
And wailing gull and shrieking shag
    Alone can pierce the ocean roar.

Unheard, a mongrel hound gives tongue,
    Unheard are shouts of little boys:
What chance has any inland lung
    Againt this multi-water noise?

Here where the cliffs alone prevail
    I stand exultant, neutral, free,
And from the cushion of the gale
    Behold a huge consoling sea.

John Betjeman
(1906–1984)

On the Sea

It keeps eternal whisperings around
    Desolate shores, and with its mighty swell
    Gluts twice ten thousand Caverns, till the spell
Of Hecate leaves them their old shadowy sound.
Often 'tis in such gentle temper found,
    That scarcely will the very smallest shell
    Be mov'd for days from where it sometime fell,
When last the winds of Heaven were unbound.
Oh ye! who have your eye-balls vex'd and tir'd,
    Feast them upon the wideness of the Sea;
    Oh ye! whose ears are dinn'd with uproar rude,
    Or fed too much with cloying melody –
    Sit ye near some old Cavern's Mouth, and brood
Until ye start, as if the sea-nymphs quir'd!

John Keats
(1795–1821)

The Sea in Summer

from: The Borough

... Turn to the watery world! – but who to thee
(A wonder yet unview'd) shall paint – the Sea?
Various and vast, sublime in all its forms,
When lull'd by zephyrs, or when roused by storms,
Its colours changing, when from clouds and sun
Shades after shades upon the surface run;
Embrown'd and horrid now, and now serene,
In limpid blue, and evanescent green;
And oft the foggy banks on ocean lie,
Lift the fair sail, and cheat th'experienced eye.
   Be it the summer-noon: a sandy space
The ebbing tide has left upon its place;
Then just the hot and stony beach above,
Light twinkling streams in bright confusion move;
(For heated thus, the warmer air ascends,
And with the cooler in its fall contends) –
Then the broad bosom of the ocean keeps
An equal motion; swelling as it sleeps,
Then slowly sinking; curling to the strand,
Faint, lazy waves o'ercreep the rigid sand,
Or tap the tarry boat with gentle blow,
And back return in silence, smooth and slow.
Ships in the calm seem anchor'd; for they glide
On the still sea, urged solely by the tide:
Art thou not present, this calm scene before,
Where all beside is pebbly length of shore,
And far as eye can reach, it can discern no more?
   Yet sometimes comes a ruffling cloud to make
The quiet surface of the ocean shake;
As an awaken'd giant with a frown
Might show his wrath, and then to sleep sink down.

George Crabbe
(1754–1832)

Cornish Cliffs

Those moments, tasted once and never done,
Of long surf breaking in the mid-day sun,
A far-off blow-hole booming like a gun –

The seagulls plane and circle out of sight
Below this thirsty, thrift-encrusted height,
The veined sea-campion buds burst into white

And gorse turns tawny orange, seen beside
Pale drifts of primroses cascading wide
To where the slate falls sheer into the tide.

More than in gardened Surrey, nature spills
A wealth of heather, kidney-vetch and squills
Over these long-defended Cornish hills.

A gun-emplacement of the latest war
Looks older than the hill fort built before
Saxon or Norman headed for the shore.

And in the shadowless, unclouded glare
Deep blue above us fades to whiteness where
A misty sea-line meets the wash of air.

Nut-smell of gorse and honey-smell of ling
Waft out to sea the freshness of the spring
On sunny shallows, green and whispering.

The wideness which the lark-song gives the sky
Shrinks at the clang of sea-birds sailing by
Whose notes are tuned to days when seas are high.

From today's calm, the lane's enclosing green
Leads inland to a usual Cornish scene –
Slate cottages with sycamore between,

Small fields and tellymasts and wires and poles
With, as the everlasting ocean rolls,
Two chapels built for half a hundred souls.

John Betjeman
(1906–1984)

Mountains, Rivers and Streams

The View from Helvellyn

from: The Ascent of Helvellyn

There to the north the silver Solway shone,
And Criffel, by the hazy atmosphere
Lifted from off the earth, did then appear
A nodding island or a cloud-built throne.
And there, a spot half fancied and half seen,
Was sunny Carlisle; and by hillside green
Lay Penrith with its beacon of red stone.

Southward through pale blue steam the eye might glance
Along the Yorkshire fells, and o'er the rest,
My native hill, dear Ingleboro's crest,
Rose shapely, like a cap of maintenance.
The classic Duddon, Leven, and clear Kent
A trident of fair estuaries sent,
Which did among the mountain roots advance.

Westward, a region of tumultuous hills,
With here and there a tongue of azure lake
And ridge of fir, upon the eye did break.
But chiefest wonder are the tarns and rills
And giant coves, where great Helvellyn broods
Upon his own majestic solitudes,
Which even now the sunlight barely fills.

There Striding Edge with Swirrel meets to keep
The Red Tarn still when tempests rage above:
There Catsty-Cam doth watch o'er Keppel Cove
And the chill pool that lurks beneath the steep.
Far to the right St Sunday's quiet shade
Stoops o'er the dell, where Grisedale Tarn is laid
Beneath that solemn crag in waveless sleep.

The golden cliffs which from Parnassus lean
With uncouth rivets of the roots of trees,
And silent-waving pinewood terraces,
And burnished zones of hanging evergreen, –
Haunts of the antique muses though they are,
May not for dread solemnity compare,
Or savage wonders, with this native scene.

Awful in moonlight shades, more awful far
When the winds wake, are those majestic coves,
Or when the thunder feeds his muttering droves
Of swart clouds on the raven-haunted scar;
And in the bright tranquillity of noon
Most awful; lovely only in the boon
Of soft apparel wrought by twilight air.

Shall Brownrigg Well be left without a song,
Which near the summit, mid the wintry snows
In a clear vein of liquid crystal flows,
And through the pastoral months in gushes strong
Gleams in the eye of sunset, and from far
Holds up a mirror to the evening star,
While round its mouth the thirsty sheepflocks throng?

And now, with loitering step and minds unbent
Through hope fulfilled, we reached the vale once more;
And, wending slowly along Rydal shore,
Watched the dusk splendor which from Langdale went,
And on the hills dethroned the afternoon;
And home was gained ere yet the yellow moon
From over Wansfell her first greeting sent.

F. W. Faber
(1814–1863)

Climbing Snowdon on a Summer Night

from: The Prelude

It was a close, warm, breezeless summer night,
Wan, dull, and glaring, with a dripping fog
Low-hung and thick that covered all the sky;
But, undiscouraged, we began to climb
The mountain-side. The mist soon girt us round,
And, after ordinary traveller's talk
With our conductor, pensively we sank
Each into commerce with his private thoughts:
Thus did we breast the ascent, and by myself
Was nothing either seen or heard that checked
Those musings or diverted, save that once
The shepherd's lurcher, who, among the crags,
Had to his joy unearthed a hedgehog, teased
His coiled-up prey with barkings turbulent.
This small adventure, for even such it seemed
In that wild place and at the dead of night,
Being over and forgotten, on we wound
In silence as before. With forehead bent
Earthward, as if in opposition set
Against an enemy, I panted up
With eager pace, and no less eager thoughts.
Thus might we wear a midnight hour away,
Ascending at loose distance each from each,
And I, as chanced, the foremost of the band;
When at my feet the ground appeared to brighten,
And with a step or two seemed brighter still;
Nor was time given to ask or learn the cause,
For instantly a light upon the turf
Fell like a flash, and lo! as I looked up,
The Moon hung naked in a firmament
Of azure without cloud, and at my feet
Rested a silent sea of hoary mist.

William Wordsworth
(1770–1850)

Summit of Skiddaw

At length here stand we, wrapt as in the cloud
In which light dwelt before the sun was born,
When the great fiat issued, in the morn
Of this fair world; alone and in a shroud
Of dazzling mist, while the wind, whistling loud,
Buffets thy streaming locks: – result forlorn
For us who up yon steep our way have worn,
Elate with hope and of our daring proud.
Yet though no stretch of glorious prospect range
Beneath our vision, – neither Scottish coast
Nor ocean-island, nor the future boast
Of far-off hills descried, – I would not change
For aught on earth this solitary hour
Of Nature's grandest and most sacred power.

Henry Alford
(1810–1871)

The Waterfall

With what deep murmurs through time's silent stealth
Doth thy transparent, cool and watery wealth
           Here flowing fall,
           And chide, and call,
As if his liquid, loose retinue stayed
Ling'ring, and were of this steep place afraid,
           The common pass
           Where, clear as glass,
           All must descend
           Not to an end:
But quickened by this deep and rocky grave,
Rise to a longer course more bright and brave.
Dear stream! dear bank, where often I
Have sat, and pleased my pensive eye,
Why, since each drop of thy quick store
Runs thither, whence it flowed before,
Should poor souls fear a shade or night,
Who came (sure) from a sea of light?

Henry Vaughan
(1622–1695)

The Prospect

from: Grongar Hill

See on the mountain's southern side,
Where the prospect opens wide,
Where the evening gilds the tide,
How close and small the hedges lie!
What streaks of meadows cross the eye!
A step, methinks, may pass the stream,
So little distant dangers seem;
So we mistake the future's face,
Ey'd through hope's deluding glass;
As yon summits soft and fair,
Clad in colours of the air,
Which, to those who journey near,
Barren, brown, and rough appear.
Still we tread, tir'd, the same coarse way,
The present's still a cloudy day.

John Dyer
(1701–1757)

Sonnet

There is a little unpretending Rill
Of limpid water, humbler far than aught
That ever among Men or Naiads sought
Notice or name! – It quivers down the hill,
Furrowing its shallow way with dubious will;
Yet to my mind this scanty stream is brought
Oftener than Ganges or the Nile; a thought
Of private recollection sweet and still!
Months perish with their moons; year treads on year;
But, faithful Emma! thou with me canst say
That, while ten thousand pleasures disappear,
And flies their memory fast almost as they;
The immortal Spirit of one happy day
Lingers beside that Rill, in vision clear.

William Wordsworth
(1770–1850)

Rivulet

By the sad purling of some rivulet
    O'er which the bending yew and willow grow,
That scarce the glimmerings of the day permit
    To view the melancholy banks below,
Where dwells no noise but what the murmurs make,
When the unwilling stream the shade forsakes.

Aphra Behn
(1640–1689)

Song

The feathers of the willow
Are half of them grown yellow
    Above the swelling stream;
And ragged are the bushes,
And rusty now the rushes,
    And wild the clouded gleam.

The thistle now is older,
His stalk begins to moulder,
    His head is white as snow;
The branches all are barer,
The linnet's song is rarer,
    The robin pipeth now.

Richard Watson Dixon
(1833–1900)

Ouse

from: The Task

Here Ouse, slow winding through a level plain
Of spacious meads with cattle sprinkled o'er,
Conducts the eye along its sinuous course
Delighted. There, fast rooted in their bank,
Stand, never overlook'd, our fav'rite elms,
That screen the herdsman's solitary hut;
While far beyond, and overthwart the stream
That, as with molten glass, inlays the vale,
The sloping land recedes into the clouds;
Displaying on its varied side the grace
Of hedge-row beauties numberless, square tow'r
Tall spire, from which the sound of cheerful bells
Just undulates upon the list'ning ear,
Groves, heaths, and smoking villages, remote.

William Cowper
(1731–1800)

The Cherwell

O silent Cherwell! once wert thou
A minstrel river; thou didst flow
Gently as now, but all along
Was heard that sweet itinerant song,
Which thou hadst learnt in coming down
From the rich slope of Helidon,
The green-capped hill that overlooks
Fair Warwick's deep and shady brooks,
And blithe Northampton's meadow nooks,
Tamest of Counties! with a dower
Of humblest beauty rich, a power
Only by quiet minds obeyed,
And by the restless spurned, – scant shade,
And ruddy fallow, and mid these
Rare meadows, foliage-framed, which please
The leisure-loving heart, and line
Where the slow-footed rivers shine,
Upon whose reedy waters swim
The roving sea-birds, on the brim
Of flooded Nenna, in a fleet
With a golden lustre lit,
What time the short Autumnal day
Sets o'er the tower of Fotheringay.

F. W. Faber
(1814–1863)

By Severn

If England, her spirit lives anywhere
It is by Severn, by hawthorns, and grand willows.
Earth heaves up twice a hundred feet in air
And ruddy clay falls scooped out to the weedy shallows.
There in the brakes of May Spring has her chambers,
Robing-rooms of hawthorn, cowslip, cuckoo flower –
Wonder complete changes for each square joy's hour,
Past thought miracles are there and beyond numbers.
If for the drab atmospheres and managed lighting
In London town, Oriana's playwrights had
Wainlode her theatre and then coppice clad
Hill for her ground of sauntering and idle waiting.
Why, then I think, our chieftest glory of pride
(The Elizabethans of Thames, South and Northern side)
Would nothing of its needing be denied,
And her sons praises from England's mouth again be outcried.

Ivor Gurney
(1890–1937)

Sonnet to the River Otter

Dear native Brook! wild Streamlet of the West!
   How many various-fated years have past,
   What happy and what mournful hours, since last
I skimmed the smooth thin stone along thy breast,
Numbering its light leaps! yet so deep imprest
Sink the sweet scenes of childhood, that mine eyes
   I never shut amid the sunny ray,
But straight with all their tints thy waters rise,
   Thy crossing plank, thy marge with willows grey,
And bedded sand that veined with various dyes
Gleamed through thy bright transparence! On my way
   Visions of Childhood! oft have ye beguiled
Lone manhood's cares, yet waking fondest sighs:
   Ah! that once more I were a careless Child!

Samuel Taylor Coleridge
(1772–1834)

The Brook

Seated once by a brook, watching a child
Chiefly that paddled, I was thus beguiled.
Mellow the blackbird sang and sharp the thrush
Not far off in the oak and hazel brush,
Unseen. There was a scent like honeycomb
From mugwort dull. And down upon the dome
Of the stone the cart-horse kicks against so oft
A butterfly alighted. From aloft
He took the heat of the sun, and from below.
On the hot stone he perched contented so,
As if never a cart would pass again
That way; as if I were the last of men
And he the first of insects to have earth
And sun together and to know their worth.
I was divided between him and the gleam,
The motion, and the voices, of the stream,
The waters running frizzled over gravel,
That never vanish and for ever travel.
A grey flycatcher silent on a fence
And I sat as if we had been there since
The horseman and the horse lying beneath
The fir-tree-covered barrow on the heath,
The horseman and the horse with silver shoes,
Galloped the downs last. All that I could lose
I lost. And then the child's voice raised the dead.
'No one's been here before' was what she said
And what I felt, yet never should have found
A word for, while I gathered sight and sound.

Edward Thomas
(1878–1917)

Low River

So high the river wont to rise
    When wintry rains his wells increase,
Now lowly in his channel lies
    That summer bids his torrent cease.

And now all day his stony bed
    Glares to the sun in ruin wide:
There pebble-heaps and wastes are spread,
    Which once were shallows in the tide.

Great boulders standing gaunt and bare
    Seem to expect their watery screen,
And cast their strong sharp shadows where
    Their dancing image late was seen.

But thread-like still comes on, glints low,
    And breaks not continuity,
The thin, persistent, glistening flow
    That makes the river river be;

And to the strewage says, 'Not long
    Shall wait my organ of fine tones,
Ere I return in volume strong
    To wake your music, wistful stones.'

Richard Watson Dixon
(1833–1900)

To the Deben

No stately villas, on thy side,
May be reflected in thy tide;
No lawn-like parks, outstretching round,
The willing loiterer's footsteps bound
By woods, that cast their leafy shade,
Or deer that start across the glade;
No ruin'd abbey, grey with years,
Upon thy marge its pile uprears;
Nor crumbling castle, valour's hold,
Recalls the feudal days of old.

Nor dost thou need that such should be,
To make thee, Deben, dear to me:
Thou hast thy own befitting charms,
Of quiet heath and fertile farms,
With here and there a copse to fling
Its welcome shade, where wild birds sing;
Thy meads, for flocks and herds to graze;
Thy quays and docks, where seamen raise
Their anchor, and unfurl their sail
To woo and win the favouring gale.

And, above all, for me thou hast
Endearing memories of the past!
Thy winding banks, with grass o'ergrown,
By me these forty years well known,
Where, eve or morn, 'tis sweet to rove,
Have oft been trod by those I love;
By those who, through life's by-gone hours,
Have strew'd its thorny paths with flowers,
And by their influence made thy stream
A grateful poet's favourite theme.

Bernard Barton
(1784–1849)

The River

from: The Borough

With ceaseless motion comes and goes the tide,
Flowing, it fills the channel vast and wide;
Then back to sea, with strong majestic sweep
It rolls, in ebb yet terrible and deep;
Here samphire-banks and salt-wort bound the flood,
There stakes and sea-weeds withering on the mud;
And higher up, a ridge of all things base,
Which some strong tide has rolled upon the place.

    Thy gentle river boasts its pygmy boat,
Urged on by pains, half grounded, half afloat;
While at her stern an angler takes his stand,
And marks the fish he purposes to land
From that clear space, where, in the cheerful ray
Of the warm sun, the sealy people play.

    Far other craft our prouder river shows,
Hoys, pinks, and sloops; brigs, brigantines, and snows:
Nor angler we on our wide stream descry,
But one poor dredger where his oysters lie:
He, cold and wet, and driving with the tide,
Beats his weak arms against his tarry side,
Then drains the remnant of diluted gin,
To aid the warmth that languishes within;
Renewing oft his poor attempts to beat
His tingling fingers into gathering heat.

George Crabbe
(1754–1832)

The Fens

There's not a hill in all the view,
Save that a forkèd cloud or two
Upon the verge of distance lies
And into mountains cheats the eyes.
And as to trees the willows wear
Lopped heads as high as bushes are;
Some taller things the distance shrouds
That may be trees or stacks or clouds
Or may be nothing; still they wear
A semblance where there's nought to spare.

Among the tawny tasselled reed
The ducks and ducklings float and feed.
With head oft dabbing in the flood
They fish all day the weedy mud,
And tumbler-like are bobbing there,
Heels topsy-turvy in the air.

The geese in troops come droving up,
Nibble the weeds, and take a sup;
And, closely puzzled to agree,
Chatter like gossips over tea.
The gander with his scarlet nose
When strife's at height will interpose,
And, stretching neck to that and this,
With now a mutter, now a hiss,
A nibble at the feathers too,
A sort of 'pray be quiet do',
And turning as the matter mends,
He stills them into mutual friends;

Then in a sort of triumph sings
And throws the water o'er his wings.
Ah, could I see a spinney nigh,
A puddock riding in the sky
Above the oaks with easy sail
On stilly wings and forked tail,
Or meet a heath of furze in flower,
I might enjoy a quiet hour,
Sit down at rest, and walk at ease,
And find a many things to please.
But here my fancy's moods admire
The naked levels till they tire,
Nor e'en a molehill cushion meet
To rest on when I want a seat.

Here's little save the river scene
And grounds of oats in rustling green
And crowded growth of wheat and beans,
That with the hope of plenty leans
And cheers the farmer's gazing brow,
Who lives and triumphs in the plough –
One sometimes meets a pleasant sward
Of swarthy grass; and quickly marred
The plough soon turns it into brown,
And, when again one rambles down
The path, small hillocks burning lie
And smoke beneath a burning sky.
Green paddocks have but little charms
With gain the merchandise of farms;
And, muse and marvel where we may,
Gain mars the landscape every day –
The meadow grass turned up and copt,
The trees to stumpy dotterels lopt,
The hearth with fuel to supply
For rest to smoke and chatter bye;

Giving the joy of home delights,
The warmest mirth on coldest nights.
And so for gain, that joy's repay,
Change cheats the landscape every day,
Nor trees nor bush about it grows
That from the hatchet can repose,
And the horizon stooping smiles
O'er treeless fens of many miles.
Spring comes and goes and comes again
And all is nakedness and fen.

John Clare
(1793–1864)

The River Mole

from: Poly-Olbion

The mother of the Mole, old Homesdale, likewise bears
Th' affection of her child, as ill as they do theirs:
Who nobly though deriv'd, yet could have been content,
T' have match'd her with a Flood, of far more mean descent.
But Mole respects her words, as vain and idle dreams,
Compar'd with that high joy, to be belov'd of Tames:
And head-long holds her course, his company to win.
But, Homesdale raiséd hills, to keep the straggler in;
That of her daughter's stay she need no more to doubt:
(Yet never was there help, but love could find it out.)
Mole digs herself a path, by working day and night
(According to her name, to show her nature right)
And underneath the earth, for three miles' space doth creep:
Till gotten out of sight, quite from her mother's keep,
Her fore-intended course the wanton Nymph doth run;
As longing to imbrace old Tame and Isis' son.

Michael Drayton
(1563–1631)

Index to Poets

Acknowledgements

John Betjeman, 'Cornish Cliffs' and 'Winter Seascape' from *Collected Poems* © John Betjeman. Reprinted with kind permission of John Murray (Publishers) Limited.

Frances Cornford, 'Country People' and 'Cambridgeshire' reprinted with kind permission of the Trustees of the Mrs Frances Crofts Cornford Will Trust.

Ivor Gurney, 'By Severn' reprinted with kind permission of Carcanet Press Limited.

Seamus Heaney, 'Thatcher' from *Door into the Dark* © Seamus Heaney. Reprinted with kind permission of Faber & Faber Limited.

Vita Sackville-West, 'Kentish Spring' from *The Land* © Vita Sackville-West 1926. Reprinted with kind permission of Curtis Brown Group Ltd, London on behalf of the Estate of Vita Sackville-West.

Siegfried Sassoon, 'Storm and Sunlight' © Siegfried Sassoon. Reprinted by kind permission of the estate of George Sassoon.

Picture Credits

Bridgeman Art/Ann Brain, Moonlit Night, 2004/Private collection: p107; Sue Campion, Stormy Sky, Pulverbatch/Private collection: p101; Gustave Baumann, Aspen – Red River, c.1925/Indianapolis Museum of Art/Gift of Stephen and Elaine Ewing Fess: p150.

Mary Evans Picture Library/Lucinda Gosling Collection: p24; The Bookshop on the Heath Ltd: p90.

TfL/London Transport Museum Collection/Catherine Alexander: p127; Dora M Batty: p88; Irene Fawkes: p114; Alfred Fontville de Breanski: p173; Clare Leighton: p134; Edward McKnight Kauffer: p153; AA Moore: pp46–47, p73, p184; Frank Newbould: p80, p120; Charles Paine: p83; Paul Reith: p188; Herbert Kerr Rooke: p64; Charles Sharland: p177; Walter E Spadberry: p19, p36, pp52–53, p59, p77, p95, pp140–141, p170.

National Railway Museum/Science & Society Picture Library/B: p26; Charles H Barker: p165; Gregory Brown: p109, p148; Austin Cooper: p182; Cusden: p144; Vernon L Danvers: p38; Paul Henry: pp30–31; Brendan Neiland: p70; Frank Newbould: p10, p14; George Nicholls: p97; Borlase Smart: p159; Clodargh Sparrow: p29; Duff Tollemache: p45; Herbert Alker Tripp: p55; Audrey Weber: p 32; Welsh: p160.